Book More Business

Make Money Speaking

PRAISE FOR
BOOK MORE BUSINESS

"The speaking business is two words: speaking and business. You could be the best speaker in the world, but if you don't understand the business, you won't get booked. And if you asked me to name the one person who could help you build a speaking business, only one person would come to mind, and that is Lois Creamer. In this book, she shares the information you need to be successful in this business; everything from the basics to advanced strategies and tactics. She gets it, and you need to get it, too!"

Shep Hyken CSP, CPAE
Award-Winning Keynote Speaker and *New York Times* Bestselling Author; Speaker Hall of Fame

"If you don't book more business, you'll never even get to the stage. Whether you're a newbie or a legend, Lois Creamer can take the business side of your business to the next level. I've hired Lois Creamer six times over the past 25 years because she remains on the cutting edge of sales and tools and techniques, and frankly, because I'm one of those speakers who is much more craft-and-speaking-oriented than sales and marketing oriented. (Sound familiar?!) Lois will give you specific and practical tips and tactics that you haven't even heard of. I promise you. I'm going to be as blunt as my hero Lois can be: If you don't book more business, then your speaking will be a hobby—not a career."

Karyn Buxman CSP, CPAE
Speaker Hall of Fame, TEDx Speaker

"As someone who always regards herself as a businesswoman running a speaking business, not a speaker running a business, Lois Creamer gets it!! I've watched in awe how Lois developed her own business, which is a model for anyone in our industry to grow theirs. She walks her talk! Her book is an extension of her business brilliance; now go get this book!!"

Mikki Williams, CSP, CPAE
Speaker Hall of Fame; TEDx Speaker; Master Chair, Vistage International

"You might be asking yourself, 'Why should I listen to Lois Creamer about how to Book More Business?' Speakers who became successful asked themselves, 'Why would I NOT listen to Lois Creamer about how to Book More Business?'"

Stan B. Walters, CSP
The Lie Guy

"Lois's book is the perfect MUST-read for those wanting to create a real career in the speaking business. As a bureau owner, I have read countless books on speaking, and this is the best strategic guide with how-tos for speakers."

Betty Garrett, CMP
Garrett Speakers International, Inc.

"I don't think there is anyone who has a stronger proven record of being the reason her clients are 'Booking More Business' than Ms. Lois Creamer. She is the real deal when it comes to professional business guidance on how to do just that. She also shares priceless information on many media platforms. The National Speaker Association, Virginia Chapter (NSA VA) believed in and loved Ms. Creamer's expertise so much she was invited back two years in a row."

Shirley T. Burke
Professional Speaker

"Up your game for instant results! Lois is extremely gifted at getting to the core of what works in growing a professional speakers business, from fine-tuning how you position yourself to how you follow up afterward. Her ability to create easy-to-use and -remember systems keeps you on track and accountable at all times. Book More Business *is a must read, and Lois Creamer is a must-have resource in your business."*

Melanie DePaoli
Professional Speaker

"Stop whatever you are doing now, because nothing is more important than reading this book! Lois Creamer is the authority on getting new speaking business!"

Jeffrey Hayzlett, CPAE
Speaker Hall of Fame; Primetime Television and Radio Host; Co-founder and Chairman, C-Suite Network; Bestselling Author

"I have been following the "Book More Business" processes for over 15 years. Lois and her wisdom and examples have helped create my one-pagers, marketing materials, telephone conversations, and my trusted Letter of Agreement. I entered professional speaking with no idea how to create or grow a business. Book More Business was my roadmap, and I still to this day continue to follow its path."

Karen McCullough, CSP
Professional Speaker

"Wow ... probably, as a professional speaker, your #1 challenge is how to book more business!! With extensive experience as a business coach, Lois Creamer 'hits the nail on the head!' No more wondering ... a great formula for MORE SPEAKING BUSINESS = MORE INFLUENCE!"

Naomi Rhode, CSP
GSF Fellow; CPAE Speaker Hall of Fame; Past President, National Speakers Association; Cavett Award Winner; 2003 Legend of the Speaking Profession Recipient; Ambassador Award, Global Speakers Federation

"There is no one, NO ONE, who knows as much as Lois Creamer about booking business as a speaker. I have reaped rewards in business, for years, after reading the Book More Business blog. Her strategies, tips, scripts work, every time. If you are in the speaking business, you are in the sales business. You have to know how to sell yourself and your services; now you can learn from the best."

Pegine Echevarria, MSW, CSP
Professional Speaker

"In today's fast-paced, data-deluged world, every second of time well invested matters! And Lois Creamer packs more value into every second than anyone else I know. I absolutely will not pass up a single encounter with her. In person, by phone, online, or in print. Her candid and practical suggestions have transformed my business. I wish the same for you. Read this book. Read it now."

Russ Riddle, CSP
Professional Speaker

"Lois doesn't tell you what you want to hear; she tells you what you need to hear. You could just book 'business,' but why not book 'more' business? Simple, effective, time-tested strategies that you will go back and reference over and over. Should be every speakers 'bible.'"

Anne M. Obarski
Professional Speaker

"Lois Creamer is a consummate professional in the speaking industry. Lois always cuts through the clutter to the essence of how a speaker can maximize their interactions to get booked more and make more. When someone asks me about starting their speaking career, I send them to Lois Creamer first. If you're new to speaking, been thinking about speaking, or have been speaking for YEARS, THIS book is for YOU!

"If you think it makes sense to invest a few dollars and hours learning how to build a profitable speaking practice and book more business, then you need to buy and read this book! Lois Creamer provides multiple no-nonsense, highly practical, and easily implementable steps you can take, starting today, that will turbocharge your sales process and increase your revenue."

Earl Bell
President, National Speakers Association - Northwest Chapter

"When a new speaker wants to ensure a very successful career, they seek out Lois. When an already very successful speaker wants to take their career to the next level, they seek out Lois. If you are either and are ready to experience an acceleration in your career, this is the book for you. Learning from Lois is truly learning from the master!"

Bob Burg
Professional Speaker; Co-author of *The Go-Giver*

"In the more than three decades of my professional speaking career, Lois has ALWAYS been the go-to person for wisdom, strategy, and kick-your-butt take-action advice. You will find practical steps, doable steps, and steps you might put on the back burner until you are ready. Consider this book your personal coach for moving your career into high gear."

Eileen McDargh, CSP, CPAE
Hall of Fame Speaker; Author of *Your Resiliency GPS*

"I've been blessed to be in the professional speaking business for a long, long time—and to have made a wonderful living and high-level fees because of my presentations. I still learn something about the industry every time I read the remarkable insights of Lois Creamer! You will too! If you want to Book More Business, then this book is a MUST read!"

Scott McKain, CSP, CPAE
Hall of Fame Speaker

"Lois Creamer is one of the most incredible strategic thinkers in the world! She has had a profound impact on my business! I can tell you without question her ideas WORK! I highly recommend you read this book! It will help you to grow your thinking and your business!"

Dr. Willie Jolley, CSP, CPAE
Hall of Fame Speaker; Bestselling Author and Nationally Syndicated Radio Host

"Lois Creamer is the consummate speaker's coach—always 'on the money' about how to start and grow a speaking business. She has the 'phrase that pays' for just about every situation. All her tips and techniques stacked end to end help you improve your marketing, sell that stalled prospect, add value to your offerings, and expand your reputation to new industries."

Dianna Booher, MA, CSP, CPAE
Hall of Fame Speaker; Author of *Communicate Like a Leader, What MORE Can I Say?* and *Creating Personal Presence*

"Genuine, authentic, life-changing, transformational, practical wisdom! That's what Lois Creamer provides for you. Her insights are so powerful that she will never ever need to market. Word of mouth ensures her business for decades to come. And you will experience the same kind of results as you integrate her concepts into your business plan.

"Uniquely, Lois successively lived out this business of speaking and writing before she ever began sharing her secrets with others. Absorb every single word within these pages. Then begin at once to implement these amazing, practical, one-of-a-kind insights. Be prepared to watch both your joy and your success escalate!"

Glenna Salsbury, CSP, CPAE
Hall of Fame Speaker; Author of *The Art of the Fresh Start*

"Lois Creamer is one of the very few authorities whose advice you can rely on. After 30 years making a comfortable living speaking, training, and coaching, I still learn from Lois. If you want to develop a highly profitable speaking practice, you have just discovered what you are looking for."

Patricia Fripp, CSP, CPAE
Hall of Fame Speaker; Past President, National Speakers Association

"Lois Creamer is the queen of practical, duplicatable systems for booking more business! Buy this book now and get busy booking more business!"

Dee Taylor-Jolley
Professional Speaker; COO, Willie Jolley Worldwide

"If you only had one resource to help you build a speaking business, this is it! Lois is a legend for a reason. Her insight and no-BS approach comes from years of real results helping speakers at all levels grow their businesses. Read her book and get busy; her brilliance will help you earn the income you want, and impact the world in the way you've dreamed."

Manley Feinberg II
Keynote Speaker and Author of *Reaching Your Next Summit!*

"The advice that Lois provides is spot on. Her wisdom and insight has helped me to book more business throughout my 20-year career as a professional speaker. If you are serious about making more money and fully leveraging your intellectual property, this book is a must read!"

Laurie Guest, CSP
Professional Speaker

"Experienced speakers and those new to the speaking profession can all benefit by reading what Lois Creamer has written about how to get ahead in this business. Her tips are easy to understand, concise, and make sense. Read this book before investing in marketing expenses and strategies to make sure they are in line with Creamer's recommendations. She knows what the speaking business is like having worked as a sales representative for a successful speaker, coached speakers, and delivered seminars."

Rosemarie Rossetti, PhD
Professional Speaker

"Duh with a hug. This is how I describe Lois Creamer's approach to building a lucrative business. She listens, asks key questions, and then points out the most obvious areas that we each avoid. Then makes you feel better for having this unknown all along and then gives you right-on-target how-tos needed to get over yourself and make money. My bank account, heart, and creative focus rely on her wisdom-based fairy dust."

Jessica Pettitt, CSP
Professional Speaker; Author of *Good Enough Now*

"When I first launched my business as a speaker, I had a lot of passion, determination—and no resources to help me build my speaking practice. Using information in Lois's blog, as well as hearing her speak, provided me with all of the tools I needed to launch my business. With her resources, I created a positioning statement. I learned how to make a cold call, write a great proposal, and discovered great advice about how to get invited back for encore presentations. Lois's book is THE go-to resource I recommend to all speakers who want to establish themselves as thought leaders and polished professional speakers."

Julie A. Connor, EdD
TED Speaker, Educator, Author

"I have been a professional speaker for 30 years, and I have known Lois longer than that. She has a special gift for working with speakers who have the passion and the message but don't quite know how to assess and increase their value and visibility. Her network is incredible. The fact that she is so much fun to work with is just an added blessing. She's the best and I recommend her wholeheartedly."

Kathleen Passanisi, PT, CSP, CPAE
Hall of Fame Speaker; Owner, New Perspectives; Author of *It's Your Life – Choose Well*

Book More Business

Make Money Speaking

Lois Creamer

Book More Business: Make Money Speaking

Published by Silver Tree Publishing, a division of
Silver Tree Communications, LLC (Kenosha, WI).
www.SilverTreeCommunications.com

Editing by:
Cathy Dorton Fyock
Barry Bronson
Mark Ray
Kate Colbert

Cover design and typesetting by:
Courtney Hudson

First edition, July 2017

Significant portions of this book first appeared,
in some format, on the Book More Business blog at:
www.BookMoreBusiness.com/Blog.

ISBN: 978-0-9991491-9-5

Library of Congress Control Number: 2017946224

Created in the United States of America

TABLE OF CONTENTS

Acknowledgements

This book has been both a work of love and the most challenging thing I've ever done. There are so many people who have played a part in the success of my life and work. I'm fortunate. I'm going to list a few of them.

Thanks to Shep Hyken, CSP, CPAE, who hired me as a business manager years ago even though I knew nothing about the speaking industry—or had even heard of a speaking industry! Shep is successful and smart, and I learned so much from him.

Thanks to my colleague and friend Cathy Dorton Fyock, who shared her *Blog2Book* book and expertise with me. I wouldn't have this book were it not for her. (I highly recommend you check her out!)

Many thanks to my clients from whom I have learned and continue to learn. I've worked with practically every type of speaker who speak on every topic in every market you've ever heard of—and some you haven't! I appreciate their trusting me with their business. I will always honor that trust.

I have too many colleagues to mention here but want to highlight a few who have been especially generous to me over the years. Karyn Buxman, Greg Godek, Kathy Passanisi, Carol Weisman, Patricia Fripp, Jeffrey Hayzlett, Jack Canfield, and Jeffrey Gitomer are but a few who not only have been supportive but have championed my business. I must also mention the late Ray Pelletier, CSP, CPAE. He gave me an incredible opportunity shortly after I started my business and always served as a mentor and friend. I think of him so often and with great affection.

Thank you to my talented and supportive team at Silver Tree Publishing, Kate Colbert and Courtney Hudson, for getting this book across the finish line.

Last but never least, my family: Dick, Maggie, Bob, Jane, Barry, Ann, and Diane. And I must include Buddy the Intern, yellow lab and Chief of Joyfulness.

Thank you!

Introduction

I wrote this book because the business of speaking is, forgive me, a really weird business. I'm betting there aren't too many friends who really get what the heck you do for a living! "You mean you talk and people actually pay you?" Heard that one?

Nothing beats standing on a stage at the end of delivering your best program and seeing a standing ovation! It's heady stuff for sure. However, in order to get to that stage, you have to put in a lot of work.

It's a weird business and a tough one. That's why I wrote this book. We only get paid when we work, and we work like heck for each and every opportunity we get. I'm convinced that the speaking business is 97 percent selling and three percent speaking on the platform. This is why I suggest you think of yourself not as a speaker, but as purveyor of intellectual property. That is the business we're really in: the intellectual property business. And the more ways you can leverage your intellectual property, the more dynamic your business will be.

Repurposing intellectual property into several different vehicles is the key to success. Speaking, writing, recording, training, webinars—these are all vehicles we use to put our intellectual property in the marketplace. Those who use them all will do well.

One of my favorite quotes in the business is from my friend Shep Hyken, CSP, CPAE. He says, "The job is not giving the speech. The job is getting the speech." True.

After years of working in corporate sales and marketing and then taking some time off to be a full-time mom, I got back into working by working with Shep. I had never even been aware of a speaking industry, but I learned the business at the feet of a master. Besides being a highly successful speaker, he is first and foremost a highly successful businessman. I wouldn't have ever started my company, Book More Business, if it weren't for Shep.

I trust this book will give you some techniques, tactics, and strategies that will move your business forward. There are now more ways than ever for speakers to apply their knowledge. I believe, however, that it starts with the speech. It starts with a client willing to take a risk (yes, a risk) of putting you in front of their employees or association members. After you hit a home run by giving a great speech, you have an opportunity to introduce the other ways you can work with your client.

But it all starts with the speech .... and with reading this book!

Getting Started

CHAPTER ONE

So You Want to Be a Speaker?

CHAPTER TWO

A Quick Start Guide: How Can I Get Started Speaking for Money?

CHAPTER THREE

Position for Success!

CHAPTER FOUR

Expert or Generalist?

CHAPTER FIVE

Public or Professional?

CHAPTER ONE

So You Want to Be a Speaker?

As you can imagine, I get approached by many who want to investigate speaking as a career. In fact, I created a product, *From Go to Pro: How to Get Started in Speaking* (see my website for purchase), just for these people. It gives the real skinny on what you need, what you'll experience, and, quite frankly, how tough it is to make a living doing this.

Now why, you may ask, would I create a product that may actually discourage people from speaking? Those of you who are doing this for a living know exactly why! It is a tough, tough business. You only get paid when you work, and you work like hell to get every opportunity.

Another reason I created this product was because I never, *never* want to be approached by anyone who can say, "Lois, you suggested I quit my job and jump into speaking!" Speakers must feel a real calling to be in the business. You have to love it to stick out lean years and hard work. Now don't misunderstand me. I think speaking is a great business, a great career—but only for some people.

Often when approached I hear, "I want to be a motivational speaker and tell my story," a story that might involve anything from coming back from the dead to climbing a mountain to overcoming a medical challenge.

It's important to have stories in your speeches; however, I tell these inquirers that they have to do more than merely tell their story. (An exception would be an entertainment-type act like a comic.) Why should someone pay you to tell your story? What will your audience learn from the telling of your story?

If you've overcome an obstacle, you must share with us the techniques you used to overcome your problems and how those same techniques may help listeners do the same. Spell out your formula for overcoming obstacles, keeping hope alive, or living with optimism.

Now to the "motivational" tag. Don't say you're a motivational speaker. If you want to use the word say, "I'm a high-content speaker who is motivational/inspirational in style and tone." That's the way to say it if you want to make money speaking! There are some great people who truly are motivational speakers, but don't assume you're going to be one of them. I'm not trying to be a contrarian (OK, maybe I am), but the market has changed. It's not the 1980s. Speakers who are known as motivational speakers and make a lot of money doing it started decades ago and have the market cornered. To newer speakers, I say simply that that ship has sailed.

As a speaker, you get approached all the time by the curious about what you do. The biggest gift you can give someone is to tell it like is. It's a hard job. It's a tough job. It's a crazy job. It's a job you must love if you are going to be successful.

And if you love it, I wish you much success!

CHAPTER TWO

A Quick Start Guide: How Can I Get Started Speaking for Money?

I'm going to assume you have a speech. If you don't, get one! If you need help, seek it out. You must have a great program that organically comes from your experience and expertise. Next, you must decide where your speech would make sense. What market could use a program like yours? Where does past experience come in? You have to make sure your program is marketable.

After you have your speech, join Toastmasters. There you will learn how to communicate in front of a group.

The next step is to get in front of groups with your program. Look for opportunities everywhere. A great place to start is with business journals and publications, regional business association websites, and social networks. They often contain calendars of upcoming meetings and programs.

Call a target group and ask if you can present your program. Don't be surprised if they give you 20 to 30 minutes. Remember, you need to be flexible! They usually do not pay; however, you'll want to ask for a testimonial letter from the leader of the group. I call testimonials the economic capital of your speaking practice. They are very important, and you should try and get one each and every time you speak.

Note: Don't use the phrase "free speech." Instead, use the term "waive my fee," as in "I may be willing to waive my fee in return for value other than money." (See Chapter 24 for more on this topic.)

Your next step is to leverage the testimonials you get into paid engagements. Note: The people who hire you and pay you don't know whether you were paid for previous speeches.

A great move now would be to see if there is a National Speakers Association (NSA) chapter in a city near you. If you want to speak, you should belong to NSA. Chapters are great places to gain expertise, meet colleagues, network, and befriend others who do the same thing you do. You can find out all about NSA and its chapters at www.nsaspeaker.org.

So, I've gotten you started. This will be the toughest job you'll ever love!

CHAPTER THREE

Position for Success!

The most important thing you can do for your speaking or consulting business, or any business for that matter, is to position it well. In doing so, you must be able to answer this question: Why hire me instead of someone else?

Begin with a positioning statement. This is defined as the concept or outcome of working with you. It is the foundation of your business. If you don't do positioning work first, you may waste a lot of time.

You can create marketing plans, materials, and web pages filled with information. However, without proper positioning, none of it is seen in context and it will never be a clear message.

My positioning statement is an example of concept and outcome marketing:

> *I work with speakers who want to book more business, make more money, and fully monetize their intellectual property.*

Isn't this more powerful than merely saying, "I consult with professional speakers about their businesses?"

Once you have a positioning statement, everything else—all content—must be congruent with that statement. Every marketing piece, website, blog post, article, consulting program, speech, and product must connect with your market positioning.

You make your life much easier once you adopt a positioning statement. It's what you say when you network, when you write, when you leave a voicemail, when you post on your social media sites, and especially when you do outbound marketing and selling to get clients. A message to a contact might start like this:

> *Sorry I missed you today. My name is Lois Creamer. I work with professional speakers just like you who want to book more business, make more money, and fully monetize their intellectual property. I'm calling to see if...*

Also, as a professional communicator, you should be able to explain what you do in an economy of words. Seven seconds or less.

In my sales program, Fast Forward Selling for corporations and associations, I suggest that you begin each sales speaking opportunity with something like this:

> *My name is Lois Creamer. I work with organizations like yours that want to fast-forward their selling skills so that they will be more successful. I'm calling to see if one of my programs may be a good fit for an upcoming meeting.*

Every time you call anyone about anything you do, open with your positioning statement. It's much more powerful than giving your name and a label like speaker, consultant, or author.

Here's a positioning statement that is used by a former Army general who now speaks on leadership:

"I work with leaders who want to stand up, step up, and take charge."

Believe me, he gets attention!

Other examples:

> *"I work with organizations that want to develop tomorrow's great leaders today."*

> *"I work with organizations that want to create a workplace environment where employees feel valued, appreciated, and acknowledged."*

If you gift yourself with great positioning, you'll reap the rewards of better defining yourself in your target markets. You'll be speaking in the language of concept and outcomes, and you'll be much better received. You'll open more doors. Isn't that what it's all about?

CHAPTER FOUR

Expert or Generalist?

Being a generalist used to be a great thing. In fact, many newer speakers still think it's a great thing. I hate to report the bad news, but that idea is so last century. The market is now seeking out experts. Speakers and consultants who go deep into one particular area instead of many are the ones in demand.

Companies seeking speakers who are generalists now typically hire training companies to come in and present, and they typically handle it through their HR departments. They are also used to paying lower fees for this type of training.

I strongly suggest that you *never* go through HR seeking a decision-maker. If you are a professional speaker and have expertise in one area, you go to executive-level people to get hired, never human resources! Further, if you start out with HR, you'll have a hell of a time getting anywhere else. In the same vein, never call yourself a trainer. Sadly, trainers are underpaid in the marketplace. If you are pegged as a trainer, you won't garner a top-notch fee.

So, a mile deep and an inch wide is my suggestion. Joe Calloway, CSP, CPAE, says it best: "Pick a lane." The reality is that clients will pay more for people who have deep expertise.

Think of it this way: Imagine a decision-maker is considering two speakers. Speaker A speaks on sales, while Speaker B speaks on sales, customer service, change, time management, and leadership.

Who do you think the decision-maker will choose if they are looking for a program on sales? He or she will likely choose Speaker A and be willing to pay more, to boot.

So, less is more in this "content is everything" market! Go targeted or go home!

CHAPTER FIVE

Public or Professional?

Are you a *public* speaker or a *professional* speaker? I see these labels all the time. I see them a lot on LinkedIn. There are groups that are called one or the other or a mix! How would you label yourself? (Perhaps you're a mutt!)

There are a lot of opinions on this question. I don't think they are interchangeable terms.

A *public* speaker is someone who speaks occasionally and typically does not receive a fee—perhaps an honorarium, but not a fee. (I don't consider an honorarium a fee. An honorarium is usually a small payment made on occasion.) Politicians are public speakers. Some executives are public speakers. Chairpersons of foundations and executives of all shapes and sizes may be public speakers.

A *professional* speaker is someone who speaks for a fee and does so as part of the way they make a living. The key here is that professional speaking is a fee-based activity where fees are received on a consistent basis.

Someone may be a public speaker who seeks out training through a group like Toastmasters, as I suggested in Chapter 2. Toastmasters is a terrific resource for speakers at any level in their career. I love Toastmasters and consider it the "Off Broadway" venue of speaking.

Many professionals like to go to meetings to try out new material. It is a great place to get thoughtful, well-considered feedback.

Toastmasters is also a real plus. You'll find professionals, but you'll also find people who are there just to learn to upgrade presentation skills they use within their companies. You'll find company executives, politicians (who really need it!), people who speak professionally, lawyers, butchers, bakers, and candlestick makers!

Regardless of how you label yourself, you need to be in the business of continual improvement. I encourage young people to take classes in communications, debate, or public speaking in school if they can. I wish this were a requirement. It will serve them well regardless of career.

Next question: How do you go from public to professional speaker? My one-word answer: SPEAK! Speak anywhere and everywhere you can. It doesn't matter if you get paid at first. You need the practice and exposure. And get testimonials each time you do.

Who to Call?

CHAPTER SIX

Target Marketing: Are You a Lobster or a Clam?

CHAPTER SEVEN

Working with Associations and Trade Groups

CHAPTER EIGHT

Good News: Your Market is Shrinking

CHAPTER NINE

Change as Opportunity

CHAPTER TEN

Market Intelligence

CHAPTER ELEVEN

Speak Nationally, Sleep Locally

CHAPTER SIX

Target Marketing: Are You a Lobster or a Clam?

There is an old joke about a woman who went to a seafood restaurant and excused herself to find the women's restroom. She encountered two doors, one labeled "Lobsters" and another "Clams." You can take it from there.

Being an "expert who speaks" is all about knowing what you deliver and the value you bring to every client. Clarity and focus—knowing whether you are a lobster or a clam—is critical. You'll need to discover exactly how valuable your information is and to whom is it of greatest value. In other words, you need to "pick a lane."

When you're starting a speaking business, you must ask yourself who would be interested in this information? Too often the reply is Everyone! But it is unlikely that everyone you call will be interested in your information.

If you want to be highly successful in the speaking industry, you need to know what industries and markets are a good fit for your information. Who values and needs your information—and has historically paid for similar information?

When targeting, ask yourself where you've had business experience—*any* business experience. What do you find interesting?

Where is your passion? Seek one or two target industries and then pick markets within those industries.

For example, if the healthcare industry is a good fit for you, then seek out markets within that industry. These might include pharmaceutical companies, hospitals, manufacturers of medical equipment, insurance companies (which can fit both healthcare and the financial services industry), uniform providers, and so on.

Years ago, I bought copies of the *Salesman's Guide to Corporate Meeting Planners* as well as the *Salesman's Guide to Associations.* Now you can get these resources on CD or online. These publications are expensive, but used editions may be found on Amazon. Even if an edition is a few years old, odds are the organizations haven't changed. The contact associated with the listing is never the decision-maker, so that makes no difference. Further, now you can access this information online with free Google searches.

My favorite resource for finding prospects is LinkedIn. They have a terrific search function, which has improved a lot over the past few years and will likely continue.

The payoff in marketing by target is obvious. Your testimonials are received more warmly. Prospects can see you have experience and can sense that if you were a fit with one group, you ought to be a fit with them. Further, if you really target, you can become a celebrity within a market. That's when you hear prospects say "Get me Joe Smith or get me a Joe Smith." You will also find you can charge more and meet less fee resistance—a beautiful thing!

So go out and target market. And if you find out who is a lobster and who a clam, let me know.

CHAPTER SEVEN

Working with Associations and Trade Groups

Everyone ready? It's time to play The Association Game! There are a lot of rules, so pay close attention. Some may be frustrating rules, but you'll be better off if you always abide by these rules. Trust me, I know from experience!

Why would I say frustrating? Truth is, marketing to associations can be very frustrating. I have sometimes referred to it as "kite in the wind marketing." Why? Because rarely will you get any chance to speak to anyone who has anything to do with decision-making. In the speaking business, that's frustration!

Marketing to state-level associations may be a little easier because most have meetings every month, although many take off summer and holiday months. This means that there are several opportunities for speakers.

When approaching state-level associations, ask for the executive director. Is he or she the decision-maker? Sometimes. If not, he or she will know who you should talk to. This is a big advantage over national-level associations.

When you speak to the decision-maker, you need to make your case. (See Chapter 16 for questions to ask.) Be aware that state-level associations pay less than national-level groups. Many speakers who wouldn't fit at the local level need to move directly to the national level. The only way to find out if state-level associations can pay your fee is to do some testing of organizations at this level. If you are constantly hearing that your fee is too high, jump directly to the national level.

When seeking out opportunities on the national level, you will rarely get a chance to speak to a decision-maker. When contacting them, ask for the meeting planner. Note: The meeting planner will not be the decision-maker, but he or she will be a person of influence. The meeting planner is the person who will ensure that your materials get on the table—in other words, considered for the meeting. Typically, on the national level, the decision is made by a volunteer committee of association members, members who you will never be able to contact. Hence the challenge. Your materials must carry the day.

The meeting planner will probably say, "Just send us your stuff, and I'll put it in the files." Many punt at this point thinking they just got the run-around. Not so. That is the process. What you want to ask at this point is, "How would you like my material to be submitted? By email or snail mail?"

After you send in your material, it's a waiting game. You'll hear if you get the job, you won't if you don't. And if you want to be considered to speak at next year's association meeting, you have to start the process all over.

See what I mean by frustrating? Then why do it, you ask? The payoff is huge! Everyone in the audience may be a good prospect to bring you in to speak. If you get the job, ask for an attendee list. Most will be happy to supply it.

When you return to your office, work the list! Call the members and say, "Did you get a chance to see my program at your association meeting? Do you think it would make sense for me to come in to your company and do a program like this?"

If they say they missed your meeting, say, "Sorry you weren't able to make it. The feedback was positive! I'm calling to see if a program like this may make sense for your company."

So that's why we play The Association Game, no matter how frustrating it is. Good luck!

CHAPTER EIGHT

Good News: Your Market is Shrinking

Celebrate when your market is shrinking? Have I lost my mind? Yes! What I really mean is, let's celebrate that the world is getting smaller and smaller due to technology. Are you with me now?

We now have all sorts of tools available to us to either give value to clients via webinars or give added value of all kinds after the speech.

I was approached several years ago to do a sales program for a corporate sales force. It would be a great job. They said they couldn't meet my fee. What to do, I asked myself? The answer was to add value after. It worked! Add value; don't lower your fee.

I asked what the plans were after my program to ensure that new ideas and strategies were applied and were actually working. Chirp. Chirp. You get it: nothing, nada, no plans at all. So I asked, "What if we had a sales meeting by phone? What if I send you a number to dial in and everyone who was at the meeting can let me know what's working, what's not, and why?"

Note that this wasn't even a Skype deal. It was the good old phone call. They took me up on it! We talked for an hour. Ten percent of the sales group took advantage of it. I got a lot out of it, and those who were in on the call did, too.

I called the person who hired me originally with a report on the call. I told him that it went well, that those who participated were chatty and happy, and that I was able to answer some questions. However, he had a new problem: an engagement problem. Only 10 percent took advantage of the call. I heard later that he had another person come in and talk engagement. Go figure!

So, what can you do that is much more sophisticated than what I did? Or, should I say, just as sophisticated as what I did? My added value took up an hour. I got my entire fee and an invitation to return. Would it work for you?

So, celebrate! Our market is shrinking. The world is getting smaller and smaller. And opportunities are getting more and more prolific.

CHAPTER NINE

Change as Opportunity

If you speak on the subject of change, leadership, or team-building, there are all sorts of opportunities you may not have considered as a fit for your business. I tweeted recently about one pharmaceutical company merging with another. Anytime you see two companies merging (and it's happening more and more), that could be a great opportunity for you.

Merging of cultures can be chaotic for companies: new people, new positions, some people losing jobs, others being transferred in, executives now becoming middle management, and so forth. It is an opportunity for you to come in and make the transition easier for everyone involved if you have expertise in this area.

Further, it may be beneficial for you to offer a package of services: Do a speech on your subject. Combine it with a consulting package where you work with specific groups within the organization to make sure things go smoothly. Perhaps offer consulting via Skype or Zoom plus a handout.

Adding consulting onto a speech is a great way to deepen the relationship, offer more expertise and, joy of joys, make more money!

I suggest my clients get a copy of *The Wall Street Journal* or access it online at least once a week on Monday or Friday. And read the business section of your local paper and perhaps subscribe to a business journal, if your city has one. Industry journals can also be good sources of information.

These are the places, along with national news, where you will hear of mergers and acquisitions. Every time you read about one, you should think about approaching the companies involved to see if you can make the transition easier. Think merging of cultures! It may be a new money-maker for you! Happy hunting!

CHAPTER TEN

Market Intelligence

I am a big believer in target marketing. You gain momentum in your marketing efforts when you work within a target industry and market. In order to be relevant in your industry, I believe you must do some market intelligence. But how? My favorite strategy comes courtesy of the terrific speaker Barbara Geraghty, CSP.

First, go to the websites of a few of the big players in your market. For example, let's say healthcare is one of your target markets. Pick some of the larger corporations that are movers and shakers in healthcare, such as Baxter Healthcare, Bayer, Kaiser-Permanente, or Cleveland Clinic.

On the home page, look for the "letter from the CEO" (or the CFO). These letters used to be included years ago when companies mailed out their annual reports to investors. Now, of course, nothing is mailed! Everything's online, including the letters.

These letters outline every challenge, key concern, and pitfall the company is facing in the coming year. It also lists the things they celebrate. We are concerned about *all* of these! When you find out the challenges, for example, ask yourself how your expertise could impact key concerns that the company or industry is facing.

For example, if you speak on employee engagement and have read that a company is experiencing a great deal of turnover, there may be an opportunity for you to help.

A great strategy to use after you have booked an engagement is to offer a pre-program questionnaire that asks your client about their business. This lets the client know that you want to ensure that your program is meaningful and speaks to any current concerns they may have.

One of the best strategies is always to keep the lines of communication open with your clients. Doing good market intelligence is smart business!

CHAPTER ELEVEN

Speak Nationally, Sleep Locally

Sound too good to be true? It isn't. I'm talking about marketing to your local convention and visitors bureau or commission. If you don't live in a larger city, pick one close to you. You may even want to belong to more than one.

I say "belong" because most of them make you join to see the goods. What are the goods? The convention calendar. It is a beautiful thing! It lists all companies, associations, and organizations coming into that city to meet, when they will be meeting, how many will be attending, where the meeting will take place, and even who the contact person is. (Don't get excited by the contact name. It's never the person to call.)

The convention calendar lists meetings of all sizes and shapes. You will even see family reunions listed. Most Convention and Visitors Committees (CVCs) only allow you to access this information if you join. There are some exceptions to the rules, so check it out.

Look at meetings that have at least, say, 75 people attending. Then go for it. If it's a company or corporation, sell to them the way you would any company. (See Chapter 10 on selling to corporations.) If it's an association, sell to them as you would any other. (See Chapter 7 on selling to associations.)

You'll want to customize your sales-speak a little. I would say something like this:

> *"I see you're coming to my hometown for a meeting. I'm a professional speaker who [insert positioning statement I helped you create here]. I live here, and you'll love meeting here! If my program would be a fit, realize there would be no associated travel expenses. If there is bad weather, it won't affect me being there on time. If I'm not a fit, keep my information handy in case you have a cancellation. If I'm not booked, I can be there fast!"*

Worst case scenario? They don't need you this year. You know this is a group that meets and so you can contact them the next time around to see if you may be a better fit. So it's in a different town? It's a great lead and could be a great booking!

Does it get better than speaking to a terrific group and sleeping that night in your own bed?

Agents, Bureaus, and More

CHAPTER TWELVE

Speaker Bureaus, Agents, and Mixed Breeds

I'm constantly asked the following questions:

- *"How can I get a bureau to book me?"*
- *"I'd like to hire someone to get me bookings and give them a percentage of my fee. Is this a good plan?"*
- *"I receive solicitation emails from companies offering me leads if I pay them a monthly fee. Is this a good deal?"*

How can I get a bureau to book me? My short answer is .... you probably can't do it on your own. Use your energy toward getting your own bookings. Bureaus are interested in working with "working" speakers—speakers who are in demand, speakers who are getting great reviews out in the industry delivering information in a compelling way.

One idea for connecting with a bureau is to see if one of your colleagues would offer an introduction for you. Your colleague will want to have seen you and really believe that what you have to offer is a fit for a particular bureau. Your friend may contact the bureau and ask his or her bureau representative to take a look at your material and see if he agrees that your information would be a fit for their clients.

Not all bureaus work with all types of businesses. This is an epiphany to some. There are bureaus that work primarily with corporations, associations, healthcare, agriculture, financial services, and more. Your program must match the bureau's emphasis and clientele. Make it your business to know who may be a fit.

Some bureaus host "speaker showcases" where they invite speakers to do 15 to 20 minutes of their best stuff in front of bureau clients and representatives. Some charge for this; some do not. This is a great way to form a relationship with a bureau. It is only effective, however, if the bureau's reps show up at the showcase. Ten years ago, these were more popular, but there still are some bureaus that do this.

Also, be aware that bureaus will expect you to provide what they call "bureau-friendly" marketing materials for them. This simply means that your contact information should not appear on the materials. The bureau wants the client to contact them, not you. You will need to make your documents bureau-friendly.

The whole "bureau-friendly" thing is a dated concept, and I've encouraged bureaus to drop it. However, some stick to this antiquated way of doing business. You need to make sure you understand how your bureau wants to handle things.

Since the advent of the internet, bureaus themselves are struggling. Any planner can search for speakers easily. Most speakers are easy to find. That said, there will always be a place for bureaus in the industry. Some companies don't want to make speaker decisions themselves and seek out those who do.

Bureaus ask for a percentage of your speaking fee as payment for getting you the engagement; the current average is 30 percent. Some speakers think this is too high and that bureaus are greedy. I don't. If a bureau brings business to your door and handles all of the details for you, I think it's worth every penny. When I hear a speaker begrudgingly paying the percentage, I say, "Don't work with them!" Bureaus can open doors that you may not be able to open yourself. If you work with a bureau, for Pete's sake, don't whine about what you are paying them!

Besides paying the bureau a percentage, you are expected to promote the bureau during your visit and to encourage the client to return to the bureau for future meetings. Also, audience members who enjoy your presentation and may want to use you are to book through the bureau. This is considered spin-off business. If not for the bureau, you would not have gotten the opportunity. You are expected to contact the bureau and let them handle the paperwork, client contact, and other details.

Some bureaus even have "exclusive rights" or an "exclusive" with the speaker. This is the same as having an agent. It means all business goes through the bureau or agent and they take their percentage. Even if they didn't get the business, if you have an exclusive arrangement, you must run it through them. I suggest to my clients that they never agree to an exclusive arrangement. It will actually cause other bureaus to lose interest in you. They will be expected to split their percentage with the other bureau, and many don't think it's worth it. Ultimately, it may cause other bureaus to stay away from you.

Because bureaus get paid by percentage of fee, they aren't interested in working with speakers who are real beginners. It only makes sense. They have to make money, too!

I encourage my clients to work with a bureau if the situation presents itself (however not as an exclusive relationship). It's a great addition to your own efforts to grow your business. You can learn a lot from bureaus about the business of speaking. I have. Some of my clients have been bureaus who hired me to work with their reps to sell speaking services more effectively.

All in all, working with bureaus can help you cast a wider net and that's what it's all about!

CHAPTER THIRTEEN

More About Bureaus and Agents

"Should I hire someone and pay them a percentage of my fee to sell my services?"

As a speaker, you may want a part-time or full-time employee to sell your services and earn a percentage of your fee. My response: Forget it!

Speakers who pay commission-only will not have a very long relationship with their employee. Lead times in the industry are shorter now, but consider this: If your employee started selling you right now, it could be months before they get a booking. Why would anyone want to sell speaking services for you based on the promise of a percentage coming months down the road? Also, this arrangement can lead to misunderstandings. Don't ask the employee to do other duties such as administrative duties if they are not going to be paid for it. In my experience, an employee hired and paid a percentage will not last long. By the time you train them and they learn your business, they will be gone.

The best scenario for a staffer? Pay an hourly fee to honor the other duties they do for you plus a percentage based on your fee. If you want an employee to really stick around, offer a year-end bonus consisting of a percentage of what the business's net profits were for the year. Doing this creates a staffer who is just as concerned with what is going out as what is coming in. You will have a real partner in your business.

What is pay-for-play? That's what I call the solicitations from companies wanting you to pay a monthly fee in return for leads. My best advice? Forget it. Most of these businesses are in the business of collecting fees, not speaking engagements or leads. Will you get some leads? Probably. Will they be quality leads? Maybe, maybe not. I have heard too many examples where they send the same leads to everyone who pays a monthly fee. This results in some poor meeting planner getting hundreds of calls from speakers asking about a meeting—a meeting that may or may not even exist. Are all companies in the business the same? No, but I have yet to hear about one that is worth your monthly fee. Next time you get a solicitation like this, ask them to take their fee out of the first booking they procure for you. You'll hear a lot of silence.

Remember, *you* are responsible for your own business growth. Don't abdicate that responsibility to anyone else.

CHAPTER FOURTEEN

Pay to Play?

Over the years several speaker bureaus approached clients to pay for "advertising." The advertising is in the form of any of the following:

- Pay to be in a catalog we are printing and distributing to our clients
- Pay to be on our website
- Pay to be featured on the homepage of our website

Note that all above begin with the words "pay to."

Don't bureaus earn their money by charging a commission on speaker fees, you ask? Why yes, they do!

I'm not a fan of paying for the things I have listed above. This was all the rage in the 1990s. When speakers started putting up websites, many bureaus lost money. They lost money because their clients could easily find a speaker on the internet. To make up for lost revenue, bureaus started charging for extra services. "Advertising," they said. I'm not a fan.

Catalog requests are mostly gone. But the plea to have a special place on the website or to be a "specially selected, endorsed speaker" is still happening. I am puzzled by this option. If a bureau feels that you are the best fit for job, THE best fit for the client, why should it matter whether or not you have paid for a special ad on their website? I've asked a few people who work in bureaus this very question, but I've never gotten an answer. Of course, I think the answer should be, "It doesn't affect choice."

As I said in Chapter 13, there's a fresh new way to approach this situation. If you are approached to do this and are tempted to do it, here is what I suggest you do: Ask the bureau to take the fee for this extra service out of the first booking they get for you! (They won't like this suggestion, trust me.)

Please understand that I don't have anything against bureaus. I love them, and you should, too. Many times, they open doors you would never be able to open yourself. You should joyfully offer a percentage for business brought to you, paperwork and details handled. (Full disclosure: I have worked with a few speaker bureaus. They have hired me to work with their agents to sell you. I think they play an important role in our industry.)

My sense is that the percentage of fee paid to a bureau, now typically 30 percent, is a fair price to pay for their services. Extras, such as advertising, should be the cost of doing business, in my opinion.

CHAPTER FIFTEEN

Hiring an Agent vs. Selling Yourself

"I'd like an agent, please."

I wish I had a buck for every time I have seen this request on Facebook, LinkedIn, and Twitter. Also, this is the most common question I'm asked when working with speakers.

My reply is, "Of course you do!" It's just not that easy. There are very few agents working with speakers, and they are working with the high-fee speakers. For the rest of us mere mortals, we really have few choices.

I have also heard, "I want to hire someone and will pay them a generous commission!" Of course you would; anyone would. The problem with this arrangement is the lead time. Rarely (if ever) when you call will someone say they are currently planning a meeting and you would be a perfect fit. When your employee starts seeking out opportunities, it may be months before anything materializes. Meanwhile, they are being paid zip. Not fun for the employee. (See Chapter 14.) Further, there are certain other administrative tasks associated with outbound marketing. They should be compensated for doing them.

Consider speaker bureaus. They approach you if interested; few want to be approached by you. The best way to get in with a bureau is to take part in a "showcase" if they offer them, or have a friend who works with them introduce you.

To work with a bureau, you have to have great positioning, topnotch marketing materials, a website, and track record of success with many testimonials and typically a fee of at least $5,000. For finding you a gig, the bureau takes approximately 30 percent.

My best advice when you're wanting someone to sell for you is to hire someone part-time to do outbound calls. They need to qualify (use my "Ten Questions to Book More Business," found in Chapter 16) and either try to book it or turn the decision-maker over to you. It's not easy finding someone to do this. And they should know your material inside and out. They should read everything you've written, watch any video, and hopefully have an opportunity to see you present in person. That's when the employee really feels invested in your business.

Is it hard to find someone? Sometimes. Consider looking for stay-at-home parents. They can do phone work while their kids are in school. Tell everyone you know that you are looking for someone part-time and that it will involve heavy phone work. Your success in business is a direct result of the amount of outbound calls that go out on your behalf. Get that? Many want a magic bullet, anything besides having to do a phone call to connect with a decision-maker. The simple fact is this: To do an adequate job of qualifying, you must, *must* have a conversation, ask questions, and get answers. You can move a relationship along with email and social media, but to qualify, to know if you are ever going to work with the prospect, you must ask qualifying questions over the phone. Your employee needs to know this. Be brutally honest about duties. Seek out someone who has been in customer service or sales.

Many speakers are seeking the services of virtual assistants. I think that's fine, but there are arrangements that are required in order to make it work. First, you must feel a strong sense of trust in this person. After all, they will be working on their own without your supervision. You must be able to share a database so each can see what the other is doing. I always suggest a weekly report using my qualifying system to tell you how many great leads you got during the week, good news, bad news, and anything else you want to include. These reports, however, should be short. You don't want any employee to spend too much time making reports.

There are a couple more questions I'm always asked connected to this: Is it better to have someone else call besides me? Does it diminish me in the eyes of the client if I'm doing my own selling? In a word ... NO! Regardless of whether you are going to have someone making calls on your behalf, you still must be the BEST at selling yourself! You should always be selling yourself along with any employee you hire.

So, you want an agent to do your bidding? So does everyone else! I feel that if you follow my advice, you may have a better shot at making progress with a salesperson. Further, if you work with me and I train them how to sell, they'll have an even better chance of success!

CHAPTER SIXTEEN

Ten Questions to Book More Business

Using a qualifying system can be a powerful tool in determining if you and the client are a good fit. I based my qualifying system on the three M's: Meeting, Money, and Motive. In order to find out whether a prospect has any or all of the three M's, you need to ask a series of qualifying questions.

My "Ten Questions to Book More Business" do just that:

1. **Does your organization use *paid* professional speakers?** Some organizations *use* speakers, but not all pay.
2. **How is the decision made regarding speakers?** You want to know if this person is the sole decision-maker.
3. **Who have you used in the past?** This may give you an idea of what topics they have historically used and how much they have paid for this information.
4. **Do you have a specific meeting date set?** You need to determine if you are available for that date.
5. **When do you begin to plan your meeting?** It is important to know when plans are made so you can make sure you are talking to them at the optimum time for securing the booking.

6. **Where will the meeting be held?** You ask this question to determine if you can offer some competitive advantage. For example, I live in St. Louis. If the meeting is going to be in Chicago, my expenses would be very reasonable. If they are deciding between me and a speaker in Los Angeles, I may get the job based on travel costs.

7. **Is there as theme or focus to this meeting?** You want to know if this is a good fit.

8. **Is there a budget I should be aware of?** Here is the money question. You need to discuss this with the prospect. Remember to talk about your fee as if your services are a commodity.

9. **What type of meeting is this?** Is it quarterly, annual, semiannual? You want to find out how many opportunities a year this prospect may have to hire you.

10. **Is there anything that I haven't asked you that you would like me to know about your meeting?** This is really a closure question. They will bring up any other questions they may have.

If you have the answers to these questions, you should be able to quantify how likely it is that you two will be working together or not.

That's it! Ten little questions that will move you from prospect to client. Now go do some prospecting!

CHAPTER SEVENTEEN

Selling Your Speech

The key to getting engagements on the calendar will be your ability to connect with those who actually book speakers. Outreach may be made in person (although rarely), phone, email, and often on social media.

You may begin your search on Google or Bing, but my favorite for this type of detective work occurs on LinkedIn, with Twitter as my second choice.

First, get clear about your positioning statement. It's important that you have one before you do the things I'm going to suggest in this chapter. (See Chapter 3 for details on positioning statements.)

A great positioning statement is the opener for any conversation about your business. Key to being successful when selling is knowing who you are, what you do, how you do it, and for whom you are a good fit. You want to be able to create a list of those who you want to approach about getting speaking gigs. (See Chapter 6 on finding target markets for your programs.)

When marketing speaking services, you will find that corporate and association markets are as different as night and day. National associations typically present one opportunity a year with a possibility for spin-off business. Corporations may have several opportunities a year.

Corporate Markets

When approaching corporate markets, ask for the vice president of sales. Eighty percent of the time, he or she is the decision-maker, so start there. Another likely suspect may be the vice president of marketing. *Never, never go to HR!* HR is the department that hires less expensive training programs from training companies.

When calling, one of three things will happen. One: you'll get the VP on the phone. Two: you'll get the assistant. Three: you'll get voicemail. Following is what to do in each situation.

If you get the VP, great! Give your positioning statement, then say, "I'm calling to see if one of my programs may be a good fit for an upcoming meeting." If yes, continue. To qualify a prospect, use my "Ten Questions to Book More Business" from Chapter 16. These are the questions that will help you to qualify and quantify a prospect's interest in you. If he says they never use professional speakers, thank him for his time and end the call quickly. The likelihood of your being the first speaker they ever pay for is low. Don't waste your time. Move on to more fertile fields!

If you get the VP's assistant, treat him or her exactly like you would treat the VP! Remember, these people are very powerful and can many times make decisions. Certainly, they are the ones who will decide whether you get a call back or not, so sell to them. Make them part of the process.

If you get voicemail, leave a detailed message. With a great positioning statement, you will know how to begin each voicemail message. The recipe for your message is:

- Name
- Positioning statement
- Why you're calling (to see if my program may be a fit for an upcoming meeting)
- Invitation to call back
- "I have something I'd like to send that will illustrate what my speech can do, but only want to send it if it is welcome. Please call me back and let me know if I can do this."

This little tweak, asking if you can send something, has increased the odds of getting a call returned for my clients.

Association Markets

The association market is tricky. It's like flying a kite in the wind because typically you will not have an opportunity to speak to anyone who makes a decision. Therefore, the person you ask for is the meeting planner and serves as the information gatherer. The decision is often made by a volunteer committee made up of association members. The planner will file your materials and submit them to the committee when they meet. Occasionally a committee member will come in with a name for the group to consider. This is why you always need to ask your corporate client if they are a member of an association or trade group. They may be helpful in getting you considered for the association meeting.

When selling to the association, you will tell them your topics and see if they would like you to submit your information and how they would like you to submit it. Your material should carry the day. Yes, they will check out videos on YouTube if you suggest, but be aware that the first thing they see is what you send. You will hear if you get the job; you'll hear nothing if you don't. And, if you want to be considered for the following year's convention, you have to do this exercise all over again; they generally get rid of information at the end of the planning process. State-level associations have nine to 10 meetings a year and meet in state capitals or major cities. If your fee is $5,000 or under, you could be a great fit here. Call and ask for the executive director and sell as you would to a private business.

A word about meeting planners. I've worked with clients who have spent thousands doing special mailings and marketing pieces to planners. Many join Meeting Planners International (MPI) and get their list of members and contact them. They wait for something to happen, and nothing does. Why? Simply because it's a rarity that a planner actually decides on speakers. They usually have to make decisions about venue, rooms, setup, logistics, and many other details. One client spent $7,000 on designing, printing, and mailing a great piece to all planners. I asked what it generated. Zero. *I* wasn't surprised; *he* was.

Many times, our first contact with people is to merely find out when they will be in a planning mode and wanting to fill slots with speakers. After you get this information, electronically tickle it in whatever contact management system you use. (I use the ACT content management system, as do many in this industry.) Getting planning dates is how to keep the sales funnels full.

CHAPTER EIGHTEEN

Productivity in Selling Speeches

In order to be highly productive doing outbound selling either by phone, email, or social media, you need to have some type of system that will tell you just how interested the prospect really is in you. I base mine on the three M's:

> **M = Meeting.** *Do they have a specific meeting date? If they don't, plans are still very uncertain.*
>
> **M = Money.** *Do they have enough to pay your fee?*
>
> **M = Motive.** *Have they used someone like you in the past, or do they seem interested in you and your information?*

Here is the system to implement further.

- If a prospect has three M's, they are the hottest of prospects! If you don't work with them on this specific program, odds are you will later. This is a *level 1* lead.
- If a prospect has two M's, this is still a high qualifier. Perhaps they have *meeting* and *money* but have yet to decide on motive or topic. This is a *level 2* lead.
- If a prospect has one M, it is a low-level lead. Typically, the one M is *meeting*; they have a date but no plans, so of course they aren't ready to talk money. I also call level 3 leads

> "people who like to get stuff for free and suck the life out of your business!"

I list the levels 1, 2, and 3 in my ACT database (contact management system) under ID/Status. This allows me to pull out each group and send an email just to, for example, level 1 and 2 leads.

Now this is productivity! Remember the levels are fluid. Perhaps a prospect is a level 1 lead but chooses someone else. Mark them down to a level 2 and proceed from there.

You should seek to touch each prospect who is a level 1 client once every 30 to 60 days. A touch doesn't necessarily mean a call. I only believe in calling a prospect when there is business to transact. By "touching," I mean keeping your name in front of the prospect. You can do this by emailing a blog post, newsletter, or tip, sending an article, forwarding a new marketing piece or information about a new program, sending a testimonial, or doing anything else that will keep you front of mind. Postcard marketing is still very effective. It is high-touch and low-tech, and if you do it, you will stand out.

If you do these things, you will really be running a speaking practice where you have prospects in the planning mode coming up at all times.

CHAPTER NINETEEN

Voicemail Hater?

Are you a hater? A voicemail hater, I mean. One of the tweets I send out periodically reads:

> *"If your voicemail messages are not getting returned, it means you suck at voicemail."*

And I'm serious!

Many speakers hate voicemail. Sure, I would rather talk to someone; however, voicemail is a reality to be dealt with effectively. How to do it?

First, you should develop a positioning statement, a statement indicating the concept and outcome of working with you. Some call this an elevator speech, but I suggest an economy of words. I think positioning statements have more impact. My clients will tell you these statements are transformational in their businesses because they always know what to say about what they do. All the time. To anyone.

Here is my script for a great voicemail message:

> *"Sorry I missed you. This is Lois Creamer. I work with professional speakers who want to book more business, make more money, and avoid costly mistakes. I'm calling to see if my services may be a fit.* (As a speaker, you would say you're calling to see if one of

> your programs may be a fit for an upcoming meeting.) *I'd love to send you something, but want to make sure it would be welcome. Could you please let me know if I can do that? If I don't hear from you, I'll try you again. Again, my name is Lois Creamer, and I can be reached at ..."*

Make sure you repeat your phone number TWICE slowly.

If you have a great positioning statement, you know how effective it is. (If your Positioning Statement needs help, review Chapter 3 in more detail.)

CHAPTER TWENTY

Staying Front-of-Mind with Decision-Makers

One of the challenges of seeking speaking engagements is how to keep your name in front of decision-makers even when they are not making decisions.

I advocate calling a prospect only when you have business to transact; therefore, I'm talking about what you can do between the time of initial contact and the time they are in a decision-making mode. The key to getting the attention you want at decision time is staying front-of-mind. How to do it?

Speaker one-sheet. The first thing to send is a great one-sheet after the initial contact. It gives your prospect an overall sense of your business and what you can do for them, as well as whom you have worked with. Your one-sheet introduces you and your work. A great one-sheet creates interest in the speaker and his or her programs. It allows the prospect to see what kind of results they can expect to receive in a certain program. (See Chapter 43 for much more on the one-sheet.)

I think sending an article or post you have written that will be meaningful to the prospect is a great way to stay in touch. I consider any writing "intellectual property on parade!" Those of you who follow me on twitter (@loiscreamer) know I send out this tweet often:

Thought leaders are writers. What have you written today?

Blog posts. You make a positive impact by writing. Blog posts are also meaningful. The posts you write can be great selling points to your prospects and great resources for your clients. Not to mention it can provide great discipline to keep on writing!

Articles. It's great to send an article you may find in a periodical. I send and tweet articles and posts from *The Wall Street Journal,* my city business journal, the *Harvard Business Review,* Flipbook, and others. Check out their websites or apps to find articles of interest or to repost on social media. I download apps on my smartphone and seek out great material that positions me with my clients and prospects.

Testimonial letters. One of my favorite ways to keep in touch is by sending PDFs of testimonial letters. One day after collecting a great testimonial in my mail, I wanted to share it with others. I sought out 10 people who I had recently contacted and decided to share my letter with them. I copied the original and wrote on the top, "I'd love to do a great job like this for you!" No cover letter. Keep it simple. If sending to a large company, write the name of the person to whom you are sending on top, but include no cover letter.

If someone doesn't recognize your name, they probably won't open an attachment in email. Remember, only email when you have permission or else add an unsubscribe button to the email.

Sending out those testimonial letters turned out to be a great idea. I got two pieces of business from sending 10 emails! I receive emails from my blog followers who have implemented this telling me it has worked well for them, too.

Negotiating

CHAPTER TWENTY-ONE

To Fee or Not to Fee?

"The Great Recession was an event masquerading as a trend."
— T. Scott Gross

Scott Gross is a thought leader and a terrific speaker. He wrote the powerful book on customer service, *Positively Outrageous Service*. He really has his finger on the pulse of what's happening in the world of customer service. I think he also has his finger on the pulse of what's happening to speakers and consultants in the new economy.

The speaking industry experienced a dramatic upheaval several years ago. There are many who are no longer in the business. Simply put, they could not hang on for better days. However, better days did come. I know, and my clients know, that things are better than they were. But there's no denying that things have forever changed.

In the early '90s, speakers knew what their calendars looked like a year in advance. Yes, a *year* in advance! Now, meeting planning may take place a *week* in advance. Speakers have to be flexible.

When I first started my business, I often quoted Connie Podesta, CSP, CPAE, who said, "Fee, flee, or free." Translated, this means either I get my quoted fee, I say, "Forget it; I'm outta here," or I waive my fee and do the program for free.

Well, times have changed. Even speaker bureaus are asking speakers to negotiate fees. Where does this leave you?

If you work with bureaus, be careful. They expect that a prospect will pay the same if they hire you directly or if the bureau brings you the business. I think it's unethical for you to quote someone a discounted fee over the phone yet expect a bureau to get full fee every time. If a bureau asks you to negotiate, it's up to you whether you wish to do so or not. Regardless, when someone asks you to *give* something, you should *ask* for something in return. (See Chapter 24 for tips.) This is, for some, an epiphany! If anyone asks you, for example, to throw in something like product, you should ask in return, "If I could do that, what else of value could you offer me?" This is a phrase that pays!

If you don't work with bureaus, I believe you have more latitude when it comes to fees. But you must always approach fees thoughtfully. If you target-market, be very careful in maintaining fee integrity. Take my business, for example. I work with professional speakers and consultants and swim in a small pond. I cannot vary my fees. People talk in my market, and I usually know what they are saying!

There are three things you can negotiate and still maintain fee integrity:

- **Time.** Would you be willing to do an afternoon session in addition to your morning program? Would you do a keynote and a breakout for your keynote fee?
- **Expenses.** Would you be willing to throw in expenses to get your fee? Maybe you could cash in some frequent-flier miles.
- **Product.** Are you willing to donate product, such as books, audios, videos, or manuals, to get your fee? Much here depends on the cost of creating those products.

So, if your business is down, what can you do about it? You can moan and groan and use the economy as an excuse for not working hard, or you can think of creative approaches to use in your marketplace. I choose the latter. I hope you do, too!

CHAPTER TWENTY-TWO

Getting Paid

I presented a program for a National Speakers Association chapter and got a great audience question: "When someone calls me for business advice, and this is what I consult on, how can I turn the call into a paid consulting job?" It is a question all of us deal with.

My answer is a simple one. I tell speakers to call me if there is anything I can do for them. If it's a quick question, I'm always happy to answer and not put them on the clock. I do this a lot. However, when I get a call that starts feeling to me like I'm doing consulting, I will stop and say, "It seems now we are getting into information that will take some time and should be on the clock. Let's end this call and set up an appointment so we can go into depth on this topic."

Never just say, "We need to go on the clock starting now." End the call and set up a specific appointment so both you and your client will be prepared. This is the most professional way to handle the situation without feeling taken advantage of or hurrying through a conversation.

It takes practice—in other words, *doing* it—to feel comfortable with this technique. Once you do it, trust me, you will kick yourself that you didn't do this long ago. As I said, it's fair, and it's professional!

So, stop talking, and put 'em on the clock! You'll feel better, and ultimately your client will feel more comfortable, too!

CHAPTER TWENTY-THREE

Let's Talk Money

One of the most challenging things for speakers is to talk about money. I hear it all of the time. When I do programs at National Speakers Association chapters, I am asked about this more than anything else.

Here's my tip: Talk about yourself and money as if you are talking about a commodity. Think of your intellectual property as your *product* (because it is!). Perhaps that will make it easier for you to ask for what you deserve, for what your product is worth.

Money is a qualifier to me. If your prospect doesn't bring it up, you need to. Don't ignore this part of the conversation, wasting time and energy only to find out you are way out of their budget. It's a mistake often made by those early in their careers.

When talking about your fee, say it confidently, joyfully, and expectantly: "My fee is $10,000 plus travel expenses. Is that a fit?" Then shut up! Wait to hear a yes, a no, or a maybe.

Here's how to respond to each of those answers:

- **If they say "yes," you're in!** You're open on that date, and they are interested in your topic. It's a beautiful thing!

- **If they say "maybe," they mean that they are unsure of their budget at this time.** You need to ask, "When will you know if I am a fit?" And be sure to follow up with them then.
- **If they say "no," you need to ask, "How far apart are we?"** This is where the conversation can get interesting! If you are far apart, there are a number of tactics you can take. You may say, "I can't accept that as my fee. I have agents and bureaus all over the country marketing me at my fee, and it would be unethical and unfair for me to undercut their efforts on my behalf." Let them argue with that! What are they going to say? Maybe "Damn you for being ethical?" This is the tact bureaus want you to take.

If you are offered a low fee, you may also take the opportunity to refer another speaker. You could say, "Would you like me to see if I can find someone less experienced who may be available?"

If you are close enough that you want to pursue the job, say, "If I could do that, what else of value might you be able to offer?" Then, listen to what the prospect has to say. (See Chapter 24 for ideas.)

So, if your idea of compensation is not an exact match, try one of my tactics and see if it makes a difference. You never know unless you try. Good luck!

CHAPTER TWENTY-FOUR

What is Value to You?

When a client can't meet your fee and you would like to work for that client, you might consider some other items of value that would make this work a value for you.

If a client can't meet your fee, you should ask this question:

> *"If I could do that, what else of value might you be able to offer me?"*

Then don't say another word. Let silence reign, if necessary! Wait. Wait to see what your prospect has to say. If the silence is long, expect the prospect to say, "What do you want?" Then be ready with an answer.

Value to each of us can be different. You have to define it for yourself. It has much to do with what you may need in your business at the time. Here is a list of what I think may be "value:"

- **Referrals.** Perhaps it's having the client offer to make three or four calls on your behalf to contacts they think can use what you do—and meet your fee.
- **A full paid speech ... later.** They must commit to booking you for a full paying engagement within a year of the date of the speech you are doing now. (Get it in writing!)

- **Recording.** Either a video or audio or both. Great video is a plus for promotional purposes, but it also may be a product! The same thing is true with audio. I think live audio makes a terrific product. I like it better than an in-studio recorded product. Don't worry about flubs; people know it's live and are very forgiving of any hiccups.
- **Barter.** Maybe this company produces something you could use.
- **Product, product, product!** Can the client purchase some of your products? Do you have books, audio, or webinars you could sell them? If you don't have product yet in your business, get it!

CHAPTER TWENTY-FIVE

Talking Money

"I hate to talk about money!" people often tell me. My reply (and I'm only half-kidding): "Then you better get a different job. Perhaps something in retail where labels with prices are used."

I've said it before: you are in an *intellectual property business*. You get paid to deliver what you create. One of the most difficult tasks you have in an IP business is to assign a price to it. One thing I know: If you aren't willing to do it, your prospects will do it for you. And they will undervalue you at every turn!

I can't tell you what your fee should be (something else I'm often asked). When I work one-on-one with clients, I do offer my advice after I know experience, expertise, and background, but I can't offer blanket statements. You can ask other speakers what they charge and gauge about where you should be. Do not overvalue! It's much better to be able to get experience speaking if your fee is reasonable early in your career.

That decided, I suggest a two-tier fee schedule. I think it gives you a little room to negotiate if you have to. (Bureaus are fond of two-tier schedules.) An example would be:

- One hour to half-day (three hours): $5,000
- Half-day to full day (six hours): $6,500

Make sure you have a sentence under the fees that says, "All fees are plus travel expenses." I think it's a good idea to spell out what you consider travel expenses in your agreement. For example, I list hotel, airfare, meals, ground transportation, and airport parking.

If you have a book, bring it up after the decision is made to hire you. Here are a couple of phrases that pay:

> *"Do you think it would make sense to have every attendee be able to walk away with the companion book to my program? If so, I can give you a generous discount!"*

> *"Do you think it would make sense for each attendee to walk away with a reminder of my visit and the importance you paid to bringing me in today?"*

It's hard to say no to either of those questions! I *want* it to be hard!

Note: If you are writing a book, it's a great idea to label it (not necessarily literally), a "companion book" to the speech. This will make it easier to sell.

Your fallback position if the client says no to pre-sell books is to offer them in the back of the room to anyone who would like to avail themselves of further information.

The Gig

CHAPTER TWENTY-SIX

Keynote, Workshop, or Breakout?

The terms "keynote," "workshop," and "breakout" are tossed around all the time in the speaking business. The interesting thing is, there is not a single definition for any of them. Some consider a keynote to be 45 minutes, some 90. Some call a workshop a half-day affair while others may call that a seminar. Are you concerned?

I am. I suggest you call everything you offer by one term: *program.* You offer programs that can run anywhere from 30 minutes to a full day (or whatever your longest program may be).

There is so much confusion in the marketplace with these terms that even the people who plan the meetings define them differently. This means that you must have the prospect define what they need and what they mean. It allows you to make sure you are selling them exactly what they need and delivering within the timeframe they request.

A cautionary tale: A few years ago I worked with a well-known speaker who shall remain nameless. He promoted himself as a "keynoter" all over his marketing material and his website. The economy was bad, our industry was suffering (it's now rebounding, mercifully), and he decided to work with me to see if I could help him come up with new ideas for growth.

Prior to working together, he sent me all of his material so I could review it. I kept noticing keynote, keynote, keynote. I asked him if, when he worked for associations, he did any breakouts after his keynote. His reply was, "No." Why? "I was never invited to do so," he said. And I replied, "And at this rate, you will never be."

I suggested that perhaps they weren't hiring him to do a breakout because he advertises only keynotes. "Maybe they believe you," I said. "You're telling them this is what you do, all you do, and they believe you." This was what Oprah calls an "aha moment!" Prospects indeed hired him for what he said he did.

We changed his materials and website, substituting the word "programs" for "keynotes." It made a difference. It made a difference in the way he talked with his prospects, and it certainly made a difference in the way they viewed his expertise. This one seemingly small step made a huge difference in his business!

Does it sound too simple to believe? It isn't! Try it. Not only will you like it, your prospects and clients will like it, too!

CHAPTER TWENTY-SEVEN

QR Codes and Profits

It's always a privilege to be asked to present at the National Speakers Association. Each time I present, whether at a national meeting or a chapter, I try to make sure I'm bringing new ideas, tactics, and strategies that can be applied immediately in a speaker's business.

At a recent NSA meeting, I introduced the use of QR (quick response) codes on business cards and marketing material. We have all seen these codes used in advertising, but I had not seen any speakers using them. There are two ways speakers can use them, as I discussed that day.

I shared a business card that had a code on the back. Anyone who scanned the code saw a video of me pop up saying, "If you have this business card, I will give you 30 minutes of free consulting. I bet I can help you book more business in 30 minutes!" I had many people take me up on this offer.

I also used two codes on my one-sheet marketing piece. One code led to video testimonials of my clients saying what they accomplished by working with me; another led to a client list. Both are good examples of how a speaker can use these codes on their marketing materials.

There are other ways speakers can use QR codes. I suggested to a client who works with bureaus to create a code-linked video that said, "I'm presenting at your meeting on behalf of ABC Speaker Bureau. They are a terrific bureau, and I urge you to contact them the next time you need a speaker. Of course, tell them you want me back, too!"

What do you think the bureau's reaction to this was? They knew that they had a real partner in the meeting business. In fact, they liked it so much they called me to say thanks! I predict a long and healthy business relationship between this speaker and bureau.

If you have written a book, a QR code can be a great way to promote it. Link to a chapter from the book, or perhaps a list of chapters, and have it lead to an order link. You've made it really easy for anyone to get a taste of the book and order it. I also tell speakers to put that chapter on the website as well.

When I see authors on talk shows like "The Today Show," the host always tells the audience that they can read a chapter from the book by visiting the show's website. Why don't you do the same thing? You can put it under a "Media" link on your website.

What other ways can you think of to use QR codes in your business?

CHAPTER TWENTY-EIGHT

And I Quote ...

I started capturing email addresses on my website when I started sending out Book More Business tips in 1999. (I now write my Book More Business blog.) My first tip was scheduled to go out while I was traveling.

I can't remember for the life of me what the tip was (except that I'm sure it was memorable to someone, perhaps my mother). Regardless, I wrote the tip and followed with a quote by that great American composer Irving Berlin. The quote was "Life is ten percent what you make it, and 90 percent how you take it."

I couldn't wait to check my email to see MY tip! And how smart my readers would think I was to tie Irving Berlin (for heaven's sake!) into the point.

My celebration was premature. After checking the email, I picked up voicemail messages. Here was the most memorable:

> *"Lois, take me off your damn tip list! If I wanted to know what Irving Berlin thought about the speaking business, I'd go to the library."* Click.

Yep, that was it. No name, no number, just that message.

Then I checked the next message. Here it is:

> *"Lois, Gitomer here. Was I a little short on my last message? Here's the point: When you quote someone else, you give away your expertise. However, when you follow another's quote with your own quote, your own thought, you bring the perception of expertise back to yourself. Bye."* Click.

Speaker Jeffrey Gitomer, CSP, CPAE, had taken me to school in a phone message! And it was a great lesson. I think of this story every time I see quotes come up on Twitter. If you look at Jeffrey's account, @gitomer, you'll notice he practices what he preaches. Now I do, too.

I take the time to put my own thought at the end of another's quote. Better yet, I've started creating my own quotes, and they have been well received.

So, what should you do the next time you want to quote someone else? Think of *WWJD: What Would Jeffrey Do?*

CHAPTER TWENTY-NINE

Making Yourself a Subject Matter Expert

As a speaker, you must be able to answer the question "What makes you a subject matter expert on your topic of choice?" In other words, clients want to know where you got your expertise, experience, ability to relate, knowledge, and hands-on experience in this area.

It won't surprise you to know that is the first question I ask when I sit down to work with a client. I need to know their answer in order to know how to position them in the market; they need to know the answer so they can talk about it when selling their speeches and creating marketing material and web copy.

Occasionally, the question becomes moot. Here is an example:

I had the privilege of working with Major General Byron S. Bagby. He had recently retired after a stellar 30-year career in the Army—his last command was as head of NATO—and he wanted to speak on leadership.

He completed my two-day consulting package, where we do just about everything you need do to jumpstart a speaking business or to take your business to the next level. Prior to sitting down with the client, I have them send me everything and anything they think would help me to get to know them and their area of expertise:

marketing material, articles, blogs, and video. If they've written a book or two, I'll even read them. When I sit down on day one, I know a lot about my client!

When the general and I sat down, I said, "Typically my first question with a new client is what makes you a subject matter expert on your topic?" We both laughed! I also said, "General, you want to speak on leadership. As you seek out opportunities, you must realize you are in for a culture shock. For many years, people jumped when you asked them to do something. Well, that's over! In this industry, you are an unknown." He replied, "Lois, you must realize for many years early in my career, I was the one jumping!" He knew exactly what I meant!

The rest of us mere mortals must be able to answer this same question. As you think about your expertise, consider where you have had experience—what types of duties you've had, what types of industries you've dealt in, what you do well, and what you don't do well. All of this feeds into expertise.

Doing this exercise yourself is tough. Each of us has a very myopic view of our own expertise and experience. I often say that's the reason why I have a business! I'm able to see these things with a perspective that my clients don't have.

When you are clear about your expertise as a speaker, it's easier to position what you do, build your brand, and know who you should be doing it for. As I've said before in this book, I'm a big believer in target marketing. Your past expertise and experience should help you decide on targets. Those who target-market have a momentum to their business.

Lastly, realize that positioning is a fluid thing. The more you work, the more experience you have and the deeper your knowledge base. A more sophisticated understanding of your topic becomes evident. Programs change; they become enhanced with new material constantly. You can leverage this into higher fees and other areas of intellectual property for your business, like products, systems, books, etc. So, ask yourself, "What makes me a subject matter expert?" And ask it often!

Oh, and as for the general? He's doing just fine, thank you! And, it was one of the privileges of my career to work with him.

CHAPTER THIRTY

Formula for Success

One of my heroes in the speaking business is Glenna Salsbury, CSP, CPAE. I first met her in 1994 and have had the pleasure of hearing her speak several times over the years. I had the joy of seeing her once as opening keynote speaker at the National Speakers Association convention. What she said in that program changed everything for me!

Simply being able to see Glenna on the platform is a teachable moment. She has such warmth, such connection, such authenticity. But she shared a formula she has used for years that really hit home with me. She gave me permission to share it with you. It's a formula for creating and organizing a speech. Here it is:

P = Point

S = Story

A = Application

Simple, isn't it? What *point* are you making? Spell it out. Tell me a *story* that illustrates the point you are making. Make the story one that is meaningful to your audience. Even better, make it a personal story so I can relate to you. Finally, give the *application*. How does this point and story apply to me, the audience member? Simple formula, awesome result!

It really makes sense, doesn't it? Point, story and application! Another great thing about this formula is that it is easy to listen to and follow if you are an audience member. That should always be a goal as a speaker.

The thing that I have discovered since becoming a fan of the formula is that it can be used when writing, too.

There you have it! Three simple steps to a successful speech, and a successful business. And thanks again to Glenna for allowing me to share this with you. Hint: If you ever get the chance to see her on the platform, run, don't walk to the auditorium! You won't be disappointed!

Other Revenue Streams

CHAPTER THIRTY-ONE

Creating Additional Revenue Streams

CHAPTER THIRTY-TWO

Should You Allow Clients to Film?

CHAPTER THIRTY-THREE

Videos? Yes!

CHAPTER THIRTY-FOUR

Keep Earning

CHAPTER THIRTY-FIVE

Do You Need a Book?

CHAPTER THIRTY-SIX

Why I Turned Down a New York Publishing House

CHAPTER THIRTY-ONE

Creating Additional Revenue Streams

As a speaker, you're really in the intellectual property business. You get paid when you deliver what it is that you know. It's all about delivering your expertise.

Years ago, many speakers did little but give speeches and write. No more.

Your first revenue stream is, of course, your speaking fee. It's the one where you make the most profit. But it shouldn't be your only revenue stream.

Products not only add to the bottom line of your business, they allow others to access your knowledge in a different way. Make an audio or video recording of your speech. Sell it as a downloadable audio or video file. People love this kind of product, and it sells!

Write a book. Books are a great way to share your intellectual property. As you approach writing, think of the old riddle "How do you eat an elephant?" Answer: "One bite at a time!"

If you aren't currently writing a blog, start now. Blog posts are more popular than articles, more popular than newsletters. Write a post on a dozen main points that you cover in a program or speech. A good size for blog posts is about 600 to 800 words. Embellish the post by adding a few stories that illustrate the point you are making. That post becomes a chapter. Repeat a dozen times, and you have a book. It's all about repurposing your information. This book is an excellent example.

If you have a book, you can also have an e-book or an audiobook. You can take a collection of blog posts, tips, and articles and create an e-book in days. You likely already have more content than you realize.

How about taking your program and creating a companion workbook to go along with it? Then you have a type of learning system, perhaps a self-led version of your program.

Maybe you have a program that could lend itself well to a licensing arrangement whereby someone else delivers your program—your intellectual property. Typically, in this type of arrangement, a percentage of the fee is paid back to you.

Record your speeches on a digital recorder and sell them. If people like what you have to say, they will want more of you. You'll gain from having speeches on downloadable files. Every product creates more interest in what you do.

It's like a tweet I've shared:

> *"blog post = article = speech = book = eBook = learning system = licensing agreement = ???"*

There is great value in leveraging your intellectual property in these ways. It's not only lucrative, but creative as well.

So, now that you are in an intellectual property business, how are you going to leverage it? Go out and create a new revenue stream now.

CHAPTER THIRTY-TWO

Should You Allow Clients to Film?

Have you found that when you present a program or consult, the client wants to film the event? It's happening more often. What is a speaker to do?

You are in an intellectual property business, and you must do whatever you have to do to protect your ownership of your own property. Therefore, I suggest that you always be prepared for this and not be surprised. How to do it?

Carry a taping agreement with you at all times. Put down a few restrictions on your letterhead and have it in your client file when you travel. I suggest you offer a simple agreement that includes the following detail.

1. Client to provide you with a master copy of the film within seven days.
2. Film may not be sold in any manner or for any reason. (If anyone is going to sell the presentation, it's going to be YOU!)
3. Film may be viewed by employees of group that hired you only, no one else.
4. Film may be used in house for a period of a year (or whatever).

5. Film may be used by you as a marketing piece, product, advertisement, or in any way you wish to use it.

Simple? Yes! I want it to be simple and not seem too off-putting to your client.

When you have your copy of the film, review it. Ask yourself:

- Would it make a good video product?
- Would it make a good audio product?
- Could you pull out clips that could be used to promote yourself on your website or on YouTube?

I think product is a terrific thing. There's nothing like turning your computer on in the morning and finding that people have ordered products on your website. I love it!

So, be prepared. If you are, you will protect your rights, and you may even make extra profit by having an agreement. At the very least, you will be positioning yourself as a professional.

CHAPTER THIRTY-THREE

Videos? Yes!

Are videos necessary? In a word ... yes! The people who hire you are demanding videos. To those of you who are not familiar with preview videos, they are four- to six-minute videos that contain clips of you on the platform.

Over the years, I have seen some great ones and some less-than-great ones. A great preview video establishes your brand. This is a simple thing to do, yet I find it is the one thing most don't do. You need to position yourself at the beginning of a video. If you do, everything else following will make much more sense.

I worked with a very popular speaker a couple of years ago. Prior to working with speakers, I like to review what they are using to promote themselves and their services. He sent me his video. Great production value! Wonderful lighting! Perfect audio! Terrific audience shots! An attractive stage with draped background in several colors! A big screen above showing the speaker! Perfect, right? Wrong!

How about letting me know what the heck you are talking about? His video was gleaned from two appearances. He had four or five self-contained clips with stories. The problem: There was no context to the film. It was a mishmash—a pretty mishmash, but a mishmash nonetheless.

When we met, the first thing he said was, "I hope you like my video; I spent over $15,000 on it!" I gulped. He saw the expression on my face and hung his head. "Oh no!" he muttered.

I told him it needed one thing, just one thing added to the beginning. It needed a positioning statement, something that defined by concept and outcome of what he did for his clients. The upshot of this story is that he took the master back to the editor and recorded a voiceover of a positioning statement we created. Voila! Everything was in context, and it made great sense! The total cost? $100.

If you are thinking about making a standard preview video, begin with your positioning statement. Then have a few self-contained points or stories. You can act as your own master of ceremonies and introduce each clip. I don't understand speakers who hire "voice talent." You are a professional communicator! Use your voice!

Make sure your video shows you delivering content within 10 seconds. A bureau owner told me this. He said when a video didn't, he pulled it and pitched it. He wanted to see platform time immediately.

At the end of the video, sum it up with an action statement, something like: "If you like what you see, I would love to work with you!" Have your video on your website and your YouTube channel.

Many speakers have several shorter video clips on their sites. These are great! However, I think a formal preview video is something you should seriously consider. There are experts who can help you put together a terrific one, or you can do it yourself.

If you have a great preview video, it will pay dividends!

CHAPTER THIRTY-FOUR

Keep Earning

I've heard this advice from financial professionals for years: *Pay yourself first!* And I agree. For those of us making a living in the speaking business, some months are easier than others.

I want you to consider this: Think of building a business, not merely a speaking practice. The difference? Think about building an equity-based business, something that can give you income long after you come in from the road.

Many speakers have diversified by adding trainers to present their licensed intellectual property. As long as your material is relevant, it can be sustaining. You could also just outright sell your intellectual property if there's a buyer—perhaps someone who you are now using as a trainer or someone seeking to expand his or her offerings.

What if, like many, your business consists of speaking, webinars, and some ancillary products created over the years? What is there to sell?

One word, my friends, one simple word: Database! If you have a good database, you can turn it into retirement income in a couple of ways. First, you can sell it outright. If you want to wash your hands of business and not deal with any details, this is a good choice.

Another choice may be to rent your database. Have you ever considered this? You could have several people working your contacts. Each time a booking comes from your list, a percentage of the fee goes back to you! Who knows? An agent or bureau could even be interested in your list. Think of your database as having equity. You may have never thought about it.

Renting your database would work as a type of lead share. You would need someone with more technical knowledge than I have to set it up to ensure you are aware when a booking from your list happens. You could have a contract written up at the beginning of the relationship to outline how and when money would be paid—paid when deposit is made, paid in the back end, or whatever you prefer.

Remember this: It does not matter if the names on the contact list are old. You are providing a lead with a company that has historically paid professionals to come speak. And you are able to tell what type of information they were interested in.

I realize I may be somewhat simplifying setting up an exit strategy. You would obviously need an attorney and an accountant to advise you. Be smart about it.

I hope that I have given you something to think about as you go about building your business. It may be worth more than you think!

CHAPTER THIRTY-FIVE

Do You Need a Book?

"Do I need a book?" I'm constantly asked this question. You see it often on the National Speakers Association Facebook page. The answer could be "yes," "not now," or "maybe."

Shall I explain?

Too often, well-meaning people advise newbies to quickly write a book so they have something to build their business around, and so they have a product right away. I think it's a horrible idea.

I recommend that you live with your material and your expertise for a while before writing a book. What you should seek to do right away is start writing a blog. That is a way to get your intellectual property to the marketplace, small pieces at a time. The magic of being effective on social media is to have great information to put out. Blog posts allow you to do just that.

As you grow your business and get more and more platform time with your expertise, you will have stories, examples, and a deeper understanding of your topic. That is what you need to have in order to be ready to write a book.

So concentrate on getting a content-rich blog established, not a book. There is plenty of time to write a book, and the book will be a better product if you live awhile with your expertise.

Once you're ready to write a book, the next decision is whether to seek out a publisher or self-publish. I always ask clients, "What is it that you want to accomplish with a book?" Simply put, if it's for exposure, you may want to look into a publishing house, which is not an easy prospect at all. If your answer is to gain exposure and make money, consider self-publishing. Your clients couldn't care less who published your book as long as it is helpful to them!

There are lots of decisions that need to be made as you grow your business. Writing a book later, rather than sooner, makes sense to me. You may decide to write a book by using blog posts, as I've done here. I urge you to get a copy of the terrific book that helped me, *Blog2Book: Repurposing Content to Discover the Book You've Already Written* by Cathy Dorton Fyock. Great title, isn't it? Great book too!

CHAPTER THIRTY-SIX

Why I Turned Down a New York Publishing House

Writing a book is something that I'd wanted to do for a long time. When I started my business, I created a manual. I pulled it a few years ago because it was out of date.

I spoke at the National Speakers Association convention in Anaheim and talked to lots of people after the program. When I finally left and returned to my room, I had an email from a representative from John Wiley & Sons, a New York publishing house. I don't know about you, but publishers rarely email me!

Joan (not her real name) told me she was in my audience and loved my program. Further, she wanted to talk to me about writing a book for Wiley. Wow! I was stunned and thrilled at the same time. In fact, I felt my head getting bigger as the day went on.

After the convention, I came home and gave Joan a call. She loved my material, my systems, my sales questions—loved it all! However, she felt writing the book strictly for speakers was way too niche. She said my material could easily apply to many other professionals, consultants, and small businesses. Eventually, she wanted the book to be about small business exclusively in order to further broaden the base.

I sent her some of my writing, and she confirmed she liked it and sent me a proposal to complete. All of this took a few months. So, there I sat with my proposal.

I'm not exactly sure what it was that made me keep putting off completing this proposal. Colleagues said I needed to get right on it, that I was nuts to drag my feet. Still, time marched on. I would practically do anything to keep me from thinking about the proposal. A few weeks later, it hit me. The reason I was putting it off was because it really was a poor fit for my business model.

I realized that if I broadened my base, no one would buy it.

Speakers want books about the *speaking* industry from me, not books about small business. Small businesses don't know me, and I would not sell many books to them. I have no credibility there.

Traditional publishers expect you to be the number-one salesman for your book. They put a lot of the responsibility in your lap for selling. They may have some marketing suggestions, but mostly you're on your own. This was another reason I didn't want to publish a book with broad appeal.

So I contacted Joan and told her that I would be forever flattered that she approached me on the project but that, after a lot of thought, I was going to self-publish instead of going with her publishing house. Her response? A short email saying: "I regret your decision."

It was a tough decision, but it was the right decision. Would I love to have a book published by a New York publishing house? Yes! Am I willing to compromise to do so? No. My clients will be better served by my writing a niche book just for them.

Growing Your Business

CHAPTER THIRTY-SEVEN
Masterminding

CHAPTER THIRTY-EIGHT
Brand X or Brand Next?

CHAPTER THIRTY-NINE
Reputation Aggravation

CHAPTER FORTY
Should You Hire an Employee?

CHAPTER FORTY-ONE
Raising Your Fee

CHAPTER FORTY-TWO
Leverage, Leverage, Leverage

CHAPTER FORTY-THREE
The One-Sheet

CHAPTER FORTY-FOUR
Putting Out a Press Release

CHAPTER FORTY-FIVE
Tweeting and More

CHAPTER THIRTY-SEVEN

Masterminding

I don't know about you, but I can't stand the promotions promising that I can "make a million." In fact, sometimes it's hard to believe the person promoting the event has ever seen a million, much less made a million.

As for me, I'm a multi-thousandaire ... and happy. Don't get me wrong, there's nothing wrong with becoming a millionaire. But most speakers and consultants are more like me in the money department. That said, I love to hang around with people who are much smarter and richer.

One of the best ways to connect with other like-minded professionals is by forming a mastermind group. Being in a mastermind group has been one of the best decisions I've ever made to grow my business. I consider my group my quasi board of directors. Truth is, I don't make a major move in my business without discussing it with the group. Call it collective wisdom or merely being a chicken, but it gives me confidence.

There are four people in my group. We all live in St. Louis, but living in the same town is less important now because of technologies like Skype and Zoom that make long-distance meetings easy yet personal.

We have been together many years, and we know each other's businesses well. In fact, several years ago I became ill quite suddenly. For the eight weeks I was in the hospital, my group was terrific. They were able to access my schedule and take care of things I could not. I would add here that my husband still doesn't really understand what I do, so I couldn't leave it up to him. Further, I wanted him to suffer along with me ... and he did!

In our mastermind meetings, we take a few minutes of personal time for updates, then we each use the time we need to discuss our issues and challenges. For example, one month I had the group review and offer feedback on a marketing piece I was creating. We've talked about problem clients and how to word contracts, proposals, and book titles—anything and everything that comes with having a speaking and consulting practice.

We do something else that many mastermind groups do not do. We refer to each other. Because our topics and expertise do not compete, we have the benefit of being able to refer business to each other.

There are some important considerations when forming a group, such as the group size. Too big, and everyone may not have time to talk about their concerns each month. Too small, and you may not gain valuable feedback. A big consideration is this: Is everyone at or near the same place or level in their business experience? If you joined a group of veteran speakers and you're a newbie, you'll be doing lots of taking and very little giving. You wouldn't have much to offer.

When you form a mastermind group, consider meeting once a month. Many groups also go on a yearly retreat and have a longer annual meeting to discuss goals for the coming year.

Owning a small business can be a lonely enterprise. You will find it valuable to have the support—the real support—of other professionals.

Do you want to grow your business and be a multi-thousandaire? Consider starting or joining a mastermind group.

CHAPTER THIRTY-EIGHT

Brand X or Brand Next?

As I've discussed before, I ask new clients to send me everything they currently use to market themselves before we meet. I believe in doing my homework before sitting down with a client.

One client—a well-known humorist—sent me everything, including her agreement. It was awful. It had the longest cancellation clause I had ever seen. Not only did it lay out what would happen if the client cancelled on her, it included a clause indicating what would happen if she cancelled on them! I couldn't believe she would even raise the specter of canceling on the client.

She agreed to change her cancellation clause to one similar to mine. My clause, like my entire agreement, is one of the simplest and most relational out there. It reads:

> *"In the unlikely event it is necessary to reschedule our work, all of your deposit (which is an industry-standard 50 percent) will be applied toward a new, mutually agreed upon date to take place within one year of the date of the agreement. All fees will be 'fee in effect' at time of reschedule."*

In both my consulting and speaking I say that I will be the easiest speaker or consultant you have ever worked with. My agreement reflects my brand!

Everything associated with your business, including your agreement, should reflect your brand. Because this particular client was a successful humorist, I said, “There is nothing funny about you in your agreement. You’re a humorist!” She agreed and made some changes. It now contains some humor, as well as a less punitive cancellation clause. It reflects her brand.

Everything you do in the market is a reflection of your brand—your agreements, bios, pre-program questionnaires, everything. This also means that as your brand evolves, so should your materials. Make sure you take the time to review and update them often.

CHAPTER THIRTY-NINE

Reputation Aggravation

One of the most important things you bring to your business is reputation—that track record of solid accomplishment that compels prospects to want to work with you. Damage to your reputation is a serious concern. It may not even be a BIG event that will send you into damage control mode. In the speaking business, every time you take the platform, you stand (no pun intended) on your reputation. Reputation is one of the key reasons you get hired.

You risk every time you take the stage. Delivering a poor performance can be damaging. So can small things like not returning calls, answering inquiries, or returning queries from a speaker bureau. Speaking is a very public business. You can make an idiot of yourself in front of literally thousands by making a stupid comment, saying something inappropriate, or not being fully prepared. We see people doing it all the time on social media.

For us, it can affect our business drastically. We lose customers and opportunities. As small business people, we won't be hiring an agency in New York to mitigate damage. We're on our own.

Several years ago, I got a call from a very desperate-sounding speaker. He was well known and very successful, but he had a big problem. He partnered with a speaker bureau who brought him 80 percent of his business. The morning after he did a program for one of their favorite clients, he got a call.

The bureau's favorite client was unhappy. The speaker, known for injecting humor, apparently wasn't careful with a couple of jokes. The client reported his humor was "careless and off color." The bureau was mad. In fact, they were so mad they broke ties with him. That's when he called me.

Ten days after that call, I was sitting in the speaker's office talking about what he needed to do to restructure his business so he would never be dependent on one bureau (or client) for the vast majority of business. It was a hard lesson, one we can all learn from.

One of the things I had him do was write a letter to his former bureau apologizing for his misstep. He didn't think he should have been blackballed by this bureau or that his humor was too off color, but I told him that didn't much matter at this point. The best action going forward was to apologize and move on. He did. To this day, he still thinks the bureau was unfair.

The next order of business was to ensure that this problem wouldn't lead to others. He also did business with two other bureaus. He was able to ask if they had heard any negative feedback on Bureau A's dropping him. They had not.

It was now time to move on, work on, and learn from what happened. I'm happy to say that that is indeed what happened. It is a cautionary tale though.

Recovery from these kinds of situations has everything to do with how quickly and effectively you deal with damage. You need to face it head on. Walk into and through the fire. You need to do whatever it takes to make a situation right.

One of my strongly held beliefs is that relationships are more important than money in the speaking business. If you do everything you can to repair a relationship, the money will follow.

We create our reputations in business every day. Make sure you are always aware of your reputation. Your business life depends upon it.

CHAPTER FORTY

Should You Hire an Employee?

A question I'm often asked is about when to hire staff. I did a Skype session with the National Speakers Association XY special interest group on this very topic. The answer: Hire staff when it's costing you money NOT to do so! Ask yourself, "What is the best use of my time?"

Other things to consider:

- **Business growth.** Are you spending all your time doing everything yourself? If your business is growing, you had better be able to handle it. Are your clients being served well? If they aren't, they will go elsewhere.
- **Positioning.** Are you putting enough time and effort into building relationships with clients and bureaus? You aren't if your business has grown and you don't have enough time to handle all of the administrivia (my word) associated with being a business.
- **Opportunity.** Do you have time to call Oprah back? Are you missing opportunities like creating new products or writing on a consistent basis?
- **Money.** Do you have time to invoice clients, get your promotional material out in a timely manner, touch base with

prospects and clients, and pay attention to your social media platforms? If the answer is no, that's a sign, my friend.

- **Guilt.** Are you constantly feeling guilty about the time you spend on business? Does your life include other activities beyond speaking? Life-work balance should be a consideration. If your business is growing, you must grow with it. A viable business is one that is never static, always changing. Are you changing with it?

Who do you bring in? I suggest you look for someone with a great attitude. You can train someone to do anything, but you can't train someone to have a great attitude. Someone with a customer service background is good. A sales background is terrific, but selling intellectual property services is very different for many.

You probably do not need someone full-time. In fact, I always suggest you *not* hire full-time. (Did I hear a sigh of relief?) Hire someone part time as an independent contractor. Add hours as it becomes necessary and makes sense.

Where do you find someone? First and foremost, make sure you tell everyone you know that you are looking! If you do decide to go part time, offer flexibility if you can. Many will consider flexibility as important as, or actually more important than, fees. Consider a stay-at-home parent. That's how I got into the business. Advertise only after you've explored word of mouth, social media, and shouting from the rooftops. If you advertise, have respondents send a one-page résumé to a special email account. Don't give out your phone number in the advertisement; you don't want to tie up your phone. You can put an ad in your local newspaper or on *SpeakerNet News*.

What to pay? Ah, there's the million-dollar question. The good news: NOT a million! The bad news: Probably more than you think. If you want to have a contractor who stays with you, make sure you are compensating him or her fairly. Do your homework and research what an executive assistant is making in your area. I think the best plan is to pay an hourly rate plus a bonus or commission. Make sure you are honoring your employee for administrative work while still motivating her to get on the phone.

Note: There are many ways speakers compensate employees. I'm not saying if you don't agree with me, you aren't being fair. I'm merely suggesting an option or two. Remember, success is NOT a solo act!

CHAPTER FORTY-ONE

Raising Your Fee

Raising your fee is one of the most challenging decisions you will have to make in your business. And, hopefully, it's a decision you will face over and over!

Many speakers take a look at their business at the end or beginning of the year and think about fees. I don't think this is a good idea. I don't want prospects and clients to think any fee decision is made according to a calendar or arbitrary date. Raising your fee is a decision that should be made based on supply and demand. It's an opportunity—a highly promotional one—to reach out to clients and remind them now how successful you are!

When you decide what your new fee schedule will look like, pass on the news to everyone. I suggest you set it up in the following way. Indicate that your new fee will go in effect in four to six months (your decision) and that any business booked during the next months will be at the fee in effect right now. By doing this, you may convince some of your prospects and clients to get on board and make a decision so they can get you before your fee goes up. This can move a decision along!

Send out a separate email to clients and prospects. Word it appropriately. Make sure you sound like this is a celebration (because it is!).

Put it in a press release. Note: I've written before that I think putting announcements about your business in press releases is a great idea. I don't even care if the release is released to the media. Have a "Media" section on your website and put releases there—not just about fee increases, but about new programs, awards, new products, anything promotional.

When it comes to raising your fees, you always run the risk that there will be some clients you will lose in the transition because they will no longer be able to afford you. Note that you will also attract clients who would never have considered you at a lower fee. No kidding! This is how the market works.

There may be an organization or two that you want to grandfather in at your old fee for a longer period of time, say a year. Some speakers do this for clients who have been especially loyal for years. The point here is that there comes a time when they have to move up with you or move on. If they need to move on, offer an alternative.

Fees are always one of the toughest issues we deal with. Once you make the decision, you must stick with it. *Celebrate* a fee increase! You deserve it—congratulations!

CHAPTER FORTY-TWO

Leverage, Leverage, Leverage

I was once a guest on a teleseminar with the fantastic Patricia Fripp, CSP, CPAE. Never being one to shy away from a difficult question, Patricia asked, "What is the biggest mistake speakers make?"

The answer was clear to me. No matter where you are in your journey as a speaker from beginner to veteran, the biggest mistake I see is a lack of leveraging. By that I mean looking at every speaking engagement you have and asking yourself how you can use this success to get more opportunities.

Ask yourself:

- Who are the client's customers?
- Who are their suppliers?
- Are they a member of an association or trade group?
- Who do they know who could use my services (and pay)?
- Where would a testimonial from this client have impact?

You may think this is obvious; I'm telling you it isn't!

A great way to have a conversation with your client about this is by doing a follow-up call after your speech. The conversation could start like this:

> *"I'm calling to say thanks again for bringing me in to speak to your group. I had a great time and wanted to make sure the feedback continued to be as positive as what I heard at the event. If you could put some of that feedback on your letterhead as a testimonial, I would sure appreciate it! If you prefer to do a testimonial on LinkedIn, that would be fine, too. I really enjoy working in your industry and would love to seek out more opportunities. May I ask a few questions?"* (See above list!)

This approach allows you to warm up cold calls! By referring to your happy client, you've created a touch point for the prospect.

So keep in mind the "L" word and leverage your way to more success!

CHAPTER FORTY-THREE

The One-Sheet

Many speakers ask me about one-sheets: "Aren't they passé?" they ask. My reply: "You only need one if you want to work."

I'm very serious about one-sheets and you should be, too. They are still your *primary* marketing piece that can be used in a number of ways, such as:

- Mailer or emailer to prospect or client
- Follow-up email to prospect
- Part of a handout, if you use one
- Information to have on a product table that people can take home
- A leave-behind on each attendee seat as a reminder of all you do
- A script for when you are selling over the phone
- A marketing piece that can make any agent sound like they know you

I think one-sheets are a great exercise in drilling down on positioning and expertise. Your one-sheet can be one-sided or two-sided. Here is the information that should be on the front:

- A business portrait photograph

- A positioning statement that describes you by concept and outcome of working with you
- Speech titles and bullets that explain the takeaways the audience gets, each beginning with an action word
- Testimonials from people who have heard you and loved you
- A blurb about yourself and your expertise, although not a long bio
- Social media addresses
- Contact information

If you do a second side, you may consider including:

- If you have a book, a picture of the book cover and a few testimonials
- A list that deals with your topic
- More testimonials
- A short blog post
- A client list
- QR codes (quick response codes) that link to client list, videos, etc.

If you have all of the above on a one-sheet, you are golden! Over the years, I have worked with a couple of speaker bureaus who have told me that one-sheets are important to them. They use them as scripts, just as I suggested above. They expect you to have one! Have it available to email and in a downloadable PDF file on your website. One-sheets make life easier for you and everyone who works with you! I can't think of one negative associated with having one.

If you'd like to see a copy of mine, feel free to email me at Lois@BookMoreBusiness.com; put "Email One-Sheet" in the subject line. You can use it as a template.

I referred to your one-sheet as your primary marketing piece. Secondary marketing pieces can include:

- A more detailed biography
- A preprogram questionnaire
- A high-resolution business photo

When you combine your one-sheet and secondary materials, you have a readymade press kit or promo kit.

Regardless of what you hear, one-sheets are here to stay. I'm glad they are because I think they make our lives easier.

CHAPTER FORTY-FOUR

Putting Out a Press Release

Many people I talk to think press releases are old fashioned and not used anymore. To the contrary, they are indeed used. The problem is, the web is inundated with them and most don't get the kind of attention we desire. So what's the answer?

I suggest that you continue to put out press releases on any news that is worthwhile. By that I mean any of the following:

- Receiving an award
- An article you wrote printed in a prestigious publication
- An article written about you and your business
- The release of a new book
- The release of a new product
- A big event where you just presented
- Anything that you feel would bring positive attention to your business

By the way, if you don't know how to write a press release, I suggest you do what I did to learn: Google "Write a press release." True! That's how I taught myself how to write a release. One main point I would make here: A press release is not long. It is short and to the point. Read examples, and you'll see what I mean.

OK, since I've already said that the web is inundated with them, where do you post your press releases? I suggest posting them on your website under a section marked "News" or "Press Room." That is where they will get read and seen by prospects that are checking you out. Further, there may be other things you want to include with press releases on this page. Highlight events you've participated in or anything you think would be promotional.

I suggest you do this now. Go back and review events and things that you have done that you could include in a press release and write it. Postdate the release and put it up!

There are services that will host your press releases. I'm not convinced they are getting the kind of attention that is worth their fee. Wire services that distribute your news releases, on the other hand, can be powerful allies if your budget can bear their distribution fees.

CHAPTER FORTY-FIVE

Tweeting and More

I remember a few short years ago telling a colleague, "I hate Twitter. No offense, but I don't care where you went for lunch!" Now you'll hear me say, "I love Twitter!" Why? Because I've gotten business directly from Twitter and you can, too!

Twitter is the most important platform for speakers. Twitter has brought me leads that have turned into business. Further, I have learned more about social media from Twitter than anywhere else.

A few thoughts on Twitter. Remember, it's *social* media. Don't use validation services; they aren't social. Don't send automatic messages to people. I'm amazed by the number of people who practice *unsocial* behavior on social media.

When I get a new follower, I check out their profile and decide if I wish to follow back. If I do, typically I will send a direct tweet thanking them for following me and, if they're in the speaking business, inviting them to let me know if I can ever be of service. If I get a follower and don't want to follow back, I don't message.

My direct tweets inviting a call have turned out to be gold. Who knew a simple invitation to call would yield business. I sure didn't in the beginning, but I'm a believer now!

On LinkedIn, I decided to upgrade. This allows me to see who has recently visited my site and allows me to send direct email to other LinkedIn members. There are also other advantages; check them out on LinkedIn. Regular email may go to a spam folder; on LinkedIn, it doesn't.

I started my own group within LinkedIn called "Book More Business: Experts who Speak." It's specifically for those LinkedIn members who speak for a living. It's a place to offer your tactics, techniques, and ideas. It's also a place to ask questions and get answers from others within the industry. Join me if you're interested.

I don't claim to be an expert in social media. I do know what has worked well for me. My two most important platforms are Twitter and LinkedIn.

What about other platforms? For speakers, I think the most important platforms are LinkedIn, Twitter, Facebook, Instagram, and Snapchat.

Remember, social media is where you show off your intellectual property! How social are you?

After the Gig

CHAPTER FORTY-SIX

Following Up

Within 48 hours of giving a speech, call the person who made the economic decision to bring you in. Timing is important. You want the great job you did to be fresh in mind. When you connect, here is your script detailing what to cover.

- I wanted to call and say thanks again for bringing me in. It was a privilege to work with such great people!
- I also wanted to make sure the feedback you heard was as positive as what I heard before I left.
- If you could put some of that feedback in the form of a testimonial, I would appreciate it! I'll send you my LinkedIn address so you can write it in that platform.
- I consider referrals to be the highest compliment. If you can think of anyone who could use my work, let me know.
- Are you a member of an association or trade group? My message would be a good fit there. Can you help get me considered for a program at that meeting?
- Do you think it would make sense (my phrase that pays!) to take a "next step" with me to ensure that the information, tactics, and techniques I talked about are actually implemented? If you do, I'd love to discuss what that might look

like. My clients tell me they feel this adds an element of accountability.

If you get voicemail, let your contact know that you'll be sending an email to ask for feedback on the event. Put the questions in an email and offer two times you are available to talk.

By "taking the next step," I mean this:

- You could do a webinar, a series of webinars, or a Skype or Google Hangout session with key leaders or sales managers that could be recorded and shared if some can't make the meeting.
- The client could buy books, recordings, or other products you have that support your message.
- You could write a series of customized blog posts.
- You could record a series of videos.
- You could do one-on-one consulting with key leaders.

I'm a big believer in leveraging each and every successful speech into additional opportunities to work with the client. This lets you go deeper than you ever could in a speech.

CHAPTER FORTY-SEVEN

Add Aftercare to Your Offerings

Aftercare is defined as "subsequent care or maintenance." When I had surgery, part of my recovery included *aftercare.* It involved a visiting nurse coming every couple of days to check in and perform any procedures that needed to be done. This got me thinking: Why don't speakers offer the same thing?

I define aftercare as a follow-up service that helps the client accomplish more than could possibly be done in a single speech. After your program, make a follow up "thank you call" within 48 hours of the event, as described in Chapter 46, and look for ways to take a "next step" with the client.

I did this very thing when I was doing sales programs, and an interesting thing happened. Several times, I made more on the aftercare than I did doing the speech! In fact, many times the speech was more like a paid showcase!

Consider this: After a client had brought me in to do a sales program, I would call and say to the decision-maker, "Do you think it would make sense for me to work with your sales managers to make sure they're applying my content?" Think about it! It's a hard "no." It's hard to say, "No, thanks. After spending thousands for your program, we don't care if the new ideas are actually implemented." I *want* it to be hard to give an immediate "no."

(Note that aftercare can apply to any topic. If you present on leadership, your work would be done with members of the management team.)

Much of what offering aftercare accomplishes is obvious. A big consideration is money. Aftercare can be a great addition to your bottom line. One of the most terrific benefits is that you become a resource for your client rather than a mere speaker!

What services could you offer on your list of aftercare services?

Summary

I hope this book has given you the ideas, structure, and many considerations you need in your speaking practice. A measure of your success will be the number of vehicles you create to take your information to the market. The days of going from speech to speech to create a living are in the rearview mirror. Seek to build a business where speaking is just one of the services you offer.

First things first. Spend time positioning your expertise. Create a solid foundation for your business. You will be expanding on that expertise for the rest of your career. Each speech, each client, each article or blog post you write will add to your knowledge base.

Treat your speaking business like a business unless it's truly a hobby. Many speakers do this as a hobby but think it's a business. Don't be one of those people.

Invest in your business. We've all heard the old saying they you have to spend money to make money.

The National Speakers Association uses four competencies to describe the business. They are:

- Expertise: Knowledge of your subject matter
- Eloquence: Your ability to communicate your expertise

- Enterprise: The skills needed to carry out a speaking business
- Ethics: The rules or standards governing the conduct of a person or members of the speaking profession

Keep these competencies in mind as you run your business. They are great areas to invest in even as you build your business. I suggest you focus on one of the above areas each year.

Check out the National Speakers Association website (www.nsaspeaker.org) and learn about the speaking profession. I suggest anyone choosing speaking as a career should belong to the trade association that represents your industry. See if there is an NSA chapter in your area. If so, go!

A note about my business: I work with speakers only on the enterprise part of the equation. I'll refer you on the other aspects but won't do them! As you may have guessed, my business is very niche. I also speak to professional speakers all over the world.

My bread and butter work is to work one-on-one with a speaker to jumpstart and most often take their business to a new level of success. You can read about all of the ways I work at BookMoreBusiness.com.

You can subscribe to my blog, which was the genesis of this book, at BookMoreBusiness.com/blog/.

I wish you years of success in this terrific, weird, stressful, joyful, and rewarding business!

About the Author

Lois Creamer is a recognized expert working with speakers who want to book more business, make more money, and fully monetize their intellectual property.

Lois has worked with the superstars of speaking as well as with the superstars of tomorrow. Some of her clients include Hall of Fame speakers Jeffrey Hayzlett, Karyn Buxman, Kathleen Passanisi, Patricia Fripp, Roger Crawford, LeAnn Thiemam, Jeffrey Gitomer, Bill Cates, Marjorie Brody and more. Others include Cy Wakeman, Tim Durkin, Russ Riddle, David Newman, Dawnna St. Louis, Julieann Sullivan, Bruce Weinstein, Lethia Owens, Manley Feinberg, Jessica Pettitt, Chip Lutz, Renee Thompson and many more!

Lois is both cheerleader and strategist. Her expertise and no-nonsense style has led her to be invited to speak at a dozen National Speakers Association annual meetings, numerous NSA winter meetings and at every NSA chapter in the United States. She has also presented at Canadian Association of Professional Speakers conventions and chapters, as well as several Global Association of Speakers events.

Publications in which Lois appears include *Forbes, Bloomberg Business, Speaker Magazine* and *The Wall Street Journal.*

For more information on her speaking and consulting programs, please contact:

Lois Creamer
Owner
Book More Business
539 Bedford Oaks
Kirkwood, MO 63122

Office: 314-374-4007

Connect with me!

Web: www.BookMoreBusiness.com

Blog: www.BookMoreBusiness.com/blog

Email: Lois@BookMoreBusiness.com

LinkedIn: www.LinkedIn.com/in/loiscreamer

Twitter: @loiscreamer

Facebook: www.Facebook.com/Loisreamer and www.Facebook.com/BookMoreBusiness

53600066R00091

Made in the USA
San Bernardino, CA
21 September 2017